VOLUME 3

BEGIN in ENGLISH

Vocabulary-Expanding
Short Stories
for
Launched Beginners

Stories by Judith Bailey

Illustrations by Carlos Lacámara

Joan Ashkenas, Editor

JAG PUBLICATIONS

Published by:
 JAG Publications
11288 Ventura Blvd.
Studio City, CA 91604
Telephone and Fax: (818) 505-9002
info@jagpublications-esl.com

Design by Words & Deeds, San Jose
Production by Jack Lanning

Printed in the United States of America

10   9   8   7   6   5   4   3

Library of Congress catalog card no. 87-81968

ISBN 0-943327-16-4

FOREWORD:
To the Instructor

One of the great delights for my high beginning students, and for me, was their discovery that they already knew enough English to read an entire story, if simply written.

Subject matter here is quite varied. There are folk tales and legends retold, human interest stories, some humor, some biography, history, plays and even a mystery. A major attribute of all of them is that they really give the student something of substance to read—a short story or play, rather than simply a paragraph or two.

It hardly needs to be argued that these days our classrooms are filled with students from a multitude of language backgrounds. But teachers, generally, are not multi-lingual. It follows then, that we teachers can help our students help themselves by becoming adept at using the dictionary. Students are provided here with a useful beginner's vocabulary, and emphasis is placed on teaching and encouraging use of the bilingual dictionary.

Not necessarily second in order of importance is that familiarity with the dictionary is basic to literacy. Although most foreign language students use bilingual dictionaries at beginning levels of their studies, some do not know how. I feel very strongly that these students should own them, and be taught to use them right away. I say this first as a foreign language student, and only second as a language teacher. Admittedly, it can be intrusive to stop and slavishly consult the dictionary for each word. But frequently, context conveys meaning, making it unnecessary to look up every unfamiliar word. This is ideal, but not always the case, and students indeed need to look up new words from time to time. There is really nothing like it for rapidly increasing vocabulary and getting on with the story.

REGARDING DICTIONARY WORK

Because I feel it is so important that students be comfortable with the dictionary, I have included at the beginning of the book a step-by-step dictionary lesson. It assumes that the student needs help with the basic concept of alphabetizing. I found that this part is very easily understood, and paves the way for the next part, "Using the Dictionary." During the lesson I work closely with the students and read along with them, pointing out the words and letters of the words they are looking up, so they may grasp the idea of alphabetical order. It may take up to an hour or so to teach, depending on the students' backgrounds, and on class size. But the rewards of this exercise will be immediately evident.

REGARDING VOCABULARY AND WORD LISTS

The vocabulary contained here is highly controlled. It includes words from the *The 2,000 Most Frequently Used Words In English,* edited by Robert J. Dixson. In this resource, the first 500 words follow the Thorndike-Lorge list. The second 500 words were derived, with some modification, mainly from the *Interim Report On Vocabulary Selection For Teaching Of English As A Foreign Language* (Palmer, Thorndike, West, Sapir, etc.). The remaining 1000 words of this list were compiled from Thorndike, emphasizing assessed needs for teaching conversation in English to primary level students.

In order to facilitate the reading and augment the word list, there has also been included vocabulary from the *Oxford Picture Dictionary of American English.* Obviously, a picture dictionary, whatever its limits, is "universal": using pictures labeled in English to serve ESL students of every language background. Nearly all of the words used in the word list, and those which are most likely to be new to some students, are found in one or both of these resources.

The beautiful illustrations that accompany the stories are also designed to convey meaning.

In addition to this, for the benefit of Spanish speakers, there has been a special effort made to use cognates. Cognates are veritable vehicles for transferring similarities: psychological frames of reference, making for real ease of comprehension.

A comprehensive word list at the back of the book indicates which words are found in Dixson's high frequency list, which in Oxford's Picture Dictionary, and which are cognates of Spanish.

Stories are told in the present tense, and in the future using "going to", since these tenses are stressed during the first year of studies. Turning them into past tense can be an exercise for students at the appropriate level. The exercises here are not strictly 'grammar work'. That remains the burden of the core text being used in class. Instead, the focus is on vocabulary expansion, with dictionary work implied, reading comprehension and discussion.

My advanced beginning students have enjoyed these stories. More than that—they have clamored for them! I truly believe yours will, too.

Joan Ashkenas, Editor

PROCEDURE

READING

It is suggested that students be allowed to read the story through silently. Then, they may re-read it to pick out the unfamiliar vocabulary. Usually, upon this second reading, much will be understood through context and by reference to the illustrations. After that, students should be encouraged to look up words independently in the dictionary. For the first story or so, you may wish to offer extra help to those students with newly acquired dictionary skills. Then, you might ask the class to follow along as you read aloud. For extra practice, students can be asked to each read a passage orally, around the room. The large illustrations preceding each story work well at this point for group discussions. They mainly depict pivotal scenes. Students might be asked questions: "who?" "what?" "where?" "when?" Or they could be asked to describe scenes in their own words, saying, "This is a…" "I can see some…"

EXERCISES

I. Vocabulary List. The words selected here for study should be quite familiar after the readings and the dictionary work. They are listed to ensure that is the case. Also, some words are used again in successive stories in slightly different contexts.

II. Definitions. (See Answer Key at back of book). A real opportunity for vocabulary expansion is in this exercise. Here, the most challenging words from the above list have been selected. For students who wish to do so, a chance is provided to explore the dictionary and learn synonyms for words they have now studied.

You may wish students to check their own work, but you may find it preferable to discuss the answers with the class as a whole, since many of the words have multiple usage.

III. Reading Comprehension. (See Answer Key at back of book.) This exercise consists of questions to be answered by referring to the story and copying the correct passage. Its purpose is for practice in writing and spelling, as well as for comprehension. As in Exercise II above, you may want students to check their own work.

IV. Discussion. Students are asked to look at pictures and, using the vocabulary, answer questions. These are especially good for paired students, but can be used for group work as well. Students should have acquired some confidence after the initial readings and vocabulary drill, to talk with others about the situations and characters.

V. Writing. After the above oral work, students are asked to perform some original written exercises: (a) to list several things about the story or characters. In answering these, some students may be able and motivated to use original language. Others could answer the questions according to their ability, in just a word or short phrase from the story itself. You will have to be the judge of individual competency. But, since enjoyment of reading is of primary consideration here, you may not want to frighten off less able students with an exacting writing requirement. Or (b) to write from dictation. For this, ask students to study a particular paragraph from the story, then close the book and write as you dictate. This might be a new activity for many. It is suggested that each sentence be repeated slowly, first all the way through, and then in short phrases. It may be necessary to read it a third time. Advise students to note spelling and punctuation, especially if dialogue is included.

AS A COMPLEMENT TO THE LAUBACH METHOD:

Begin in English, though designed for non-English-speaking students, can also be used effectively by English speakers for remedial work in basic reading, writing and spelling. It is particularly appropriate for students of the Laubach Method at Skill Book levels 2 and 3. This book's added dimension is that it teaches and encourages use of the foreign student's own bilingual dictionary, or the native speaker's English dictionary.

A great number of the chart-listed skills at levels 2 and 3 are again introduced or reinforced here. The exercises test reading comprehension, and offer practice in spelling. Writing practice is provided, sometimes by dictation, sometimes by copying sentences for reinforcement, sometimes by referring to the text, other times in original sentences, as individual abilities allow.

The underlying intent here is, as in the Laubach Method, motivation of independent learning with a minimum of teaching help.

CONTENTS

Learning to Use the Dictionary

I. ALPHABETIZING

Use the alphabet to help you do the following exercises.

a b c d e f g h i j k l m n o p q r s t u v w x y z

1. Put these letters in correct order:

b c a _____ _____ _____

i g h _____ _____ _____

o m n _____ _____ _____

2. Put these words in correct order according to their first letters:

| sit | baby | light | house | _____ _____ _____ _____ |
| fast | apple | cake | down | _____ _____ _____ _____ |

3. These words have the same first letter. Arrange them according to their second letters:

buy	big	boy	black	_____ _____ _____ _____
pin	pan	put	pet	_____ _____ _____ _____
shell	sell	spell	same	_____ _____ _____ _____

4. These words begin with the same two letters. Put them in order according to their third letters:

plan	plum	plot	_____ _____ _____
flock	flake	flute	_____ _____ _____
street	stamp	stop	_____ _____ _____
through	thought	thin	_____ _____ _____

II. USING THE DICTIONARY

Open the dictionary to where the letter 'b' begins. Notice that the first words you see following the 'b' all have 'a' for their second letter. Now look at their third letter. Notice that these third letters follow in alphabetical order: first 'a', then 'b', then 'c', through the rest of the alphabet. Using this idea, let's practice and look up the following words: baby, back, bad, bag.

Now turn the pages and pass the letters 'ba' until you find words beginning with 'be.' Look up these words: beach, bed, before, begin.

Now continue turning pages until you find words starting with 'bi.' Find these words: bicycle, big, bill, bird.

Now look for these words: black, boat, brake, bud.

III. DICTIONARY WORK

Open the dictionary and look at the top of any page. You can see two words in dark letters. The word on the left gives you the first word on the page. The word on the right gives you the last word on the page, and between these, all words are in alphabetical order, according to their second, third, fourth, etc. letters.

Let's practice finding some words. Turn to the letter 'b' and look for the word 'bad.' You know it is close to the beginning of the 'b' because its second letter is 'a.' It comes after words beginning with 'bab' and 'bac' because 'b' and 'c' come before 'd' in the alphabet.

Let's try another word. Turn to the letter 'n' and find the word 'not.' The second letter, 'o', of 'not' is more towards the middle of the alphabet, so you must pass words beginning with 'na', 'ne', 'ni', and find words beginning with 'no'. Now you need to find the third letter, 't', after the 'o'. Look for it in its alphabetical order at the top of the pages in dark letters.

Using what you know, you can now look up any new words in the dictionary as you read.

"Is the soup too hot? I can blow on it and make it cool."

A Big Bowl of Menudo
A Play

THE CHARACTERS: Paco, the owner of a Mexican restaurant
Fay, a new waitress
Dr. Ruiz, a dentist

THE SCENE: *The dining room of Paco's restaurant in Los Angeles. It is still early, eleven-thirty in the morning. There are as yet no customers for lunch. Paco uses this opportunity to teach Fay her new job. Fay has no experience as a waitress but is eager to learn.*

PACO: . . . so you put salt and pepper on every table. But you only serve water if the customer asks for it. We don't want to waste water.

FAY: Okay, only if they ask. What about napkins?

PACO: Napkins? Of course. On every table. Oh, before I forget, this is Friday. On Fridays, our first lunch customer is always Dr. Ruiz. He's a nice man and a good dentist, but he can be difficult. When he comes in, *(Paco looks at his watch.)* which is going to happen in just a few minutes, put him at that table. *(points)* That's where he likes to sit. You don't have to give him a menu. The only thing he ever orders is a big bowl of menudo. He loves it.

FAY: What's menudo?

PACO: You don't know what menudo is? I can't believe it. It's a very popular Mexican soup. It's made with vegetables and tripe and —

FAY: *(interrupts)* What's tripe?

PACO: You don't know? Tripe is meat. It comes from the stomach of a cow.

FAY: *(she looks a little sick)* Thanks, Paco. Don't tell me any more.

PACO: *(notices something through the restaurant window)* I don't have time to tell you any more. Here comes Dr. Ruiz now, hungry as a bear. I'm going back to the kitchen. Good luck, Fay.

DR. RUIZ: *(enters and sits at his usual table, smiles at the new waitress)* Good morning.

FAY:	Good morning, Sir. I think I know what you want. A bowl of menudo, right?
DR. RUIZ:	*(corrects her)* Wrong. A *big* bowl of menudo.
FAY:	*(shouts into the kitchen)* One big bowl of menudo!
PACO:	*(answers from the kitchen)* One big bowl of menudo, coming up!
FAY:	*(goes back, picks up the bowl, then carefully puts the soup in front of Dr. Ruiz)* There you are, Sir. Enjoy. *(She waits for him to begin eating, but he does not. He just sits, looking at his bowl. Fay is worried.)* Sir, is there something wrong with the soup?
DR. RUIZ:	*(unhappy)* Taste it!
FAY:	Thanks, I don't want to taste it. Just tell me, is the soup too cold? I can take it back to the kitchen and warm it up.
DR. RUIZ:	*(quite unhappy)* Taste it, please!
FAY:	Maybe you want salt? Pepper? Here they are on the table right in front of you.
DR. RUIZ:	*(very unhappy)* Lady, all I'm asking is that you taste the soup!
PACO:	*(steps out of the kitchen to see what's going on)* Dr. Ruiz, what's the matter? You don't like my menudo any more? *(Dr. Ruiz pays no attention to Paco. He continues to look at Fay angrily.)*
FAY:	Why don't you tell me what's wrong with the soup? If it's too hot, I can blow on it and make it cool. Whatever it is, I can fix it.
DR. RUIZ:	*(shouting)* JUST ... TASTE ... THE ... SOUP!
PACO:	Fay, do me a favor. Taste it. It's not going to kill you.
FAY:	Okay, okay, I'm going to taste it. *(She looks on the table for a spoon.)* I can't. There is no spoon.
DR. RUIZ:	THAT ... IS ... EXACTLY ... MY ... POINT ... THERE ... IS ... NO ... SPOON!!!

EXERCISES

I. VOCABULARY

You probably know many of these words from reading the story and looking at the pictures. If there are still some you don't know, look them up in your dictionary now.

customer	popular	order	pepper
stomach	opportunity	experience	taste
waste	interrupt	bowl	menu
front	eager	enter	

II. DEFINITIONS

Try to guess the best definition for these words. Then look them up in your dictionary and draw a circle around the answer.

1. customer
   a. someone who buys
   b. someone who sells
   c. something that is usual

2. waste
   a. a part of the body
   b. use without being careful
   c. eat or drink a little

3. popular
   a. a kind of tree
   b. full of people
   c. liked by many

4. order
   a. a smell
   b. tell a waiter or waitress what you want
   c. an edge

5. taste
   a. stick one thing to another
   b. use without being careful
   c. eat or drink a little

6. enter
   a. come in
   b. the middle
   c. between

15

III. READING COMPREHENSION

Read the questions. Find the answers in the story. Write the answers under the questions.

1. Why does Paco have to tell Fay what to put on the tables in the restaurant?

_____

_____

2. Why does Paco tell Fay that she doesn't have to give Dr. Ruiz a menu?

_____

_____

3. How does Paco describe Dr. Ruiz?

_____

_____

4. After she serves Dr. Ruiz, Fay is worried. Why?

_____

_____

5. What does Dr. Ruiz want Fay to do to the soup?

_____

_____

6. Fay finally agrees to taste the soup but can't. Why?

_____

_____

IV. DISCUSSION

Look at the pictures. Talk to your
partner. Use words from the story.

Picture #1
Why are there no customers
in the restaurant?
Whom does Paco see walking
toward the restaurant?
Is Paco expecting Dr. Ruiz?
Why?

Picture #2
Where is Paco in this picture?
What is he giving to Fay to
serve to Dr. Ruiz?
Do you think Fay would like
to eat some menudo? Give
reasons for your answer.

V. WRITING

Write four questions that Fay asks Dr. Ruiz when she discovers he is not eating his
soup.

1. _____

2. _____

3. _____

4. _____

One of the patients, a tiny old woman in a pink raincoat and a yellow rainhat, returns with a big black umbrella.

18

The Flat Tire

Arthur Shaw is driving on a lonely country road. He stops to study his map one more time. There is no doubt about it: he is lost. He is lost on a no-name dirt road in northern Kansas. There isn't another car or a house that he can see. There is nothing but corn fields.

Art is an insurance salesman. He is just starting this job and he is in Kansas for the first time. He thinks he has a good chance to sell insurance to a farmer who lives somewhere near here. But where?

He makes a U-turn and drives back. After a few miles he notices that the dirt road crosses a divided highway. He looks for a sign telling what highway it is, but can't find one. Art wonders what to do. Go left? Go right? He decides it doesn't matter: a good road like this must go somewhere. He turns right, then looks at his watch. He has an appointment with the farmer who may buy insurance and he doesn't want to be late.

"At least this is a nice smooth road," Art tells himself, "so I can drive faster." Just then the car begins to make a funny noise. It goes bump, bump, bumping along. Art recognizes the sound: he has a flat tire.

"Oh, no!" he cries. "Not here! Not in the middle of nowhere!"

When he gets out of the car he sees that he isn't exactly in the middle of nowhere. On one side of the road there are fields of corn. But on the other side there are several large, red brick buildings. Around the buildings are gardens with flowers, grass, paths and benches. There is also a high fence, a locked gate, and a sign that says, "**KANSAS STATE MENTAL HOSPITAL**."

"You better start doing things **right**," Art warns himself, "or this is where the doctors are going to put **you**!"

He tries to remember the right way to change a tire. "First," he reminds himself, "you take off the hub cap or wheel cover. Then you loosen and unscrew the lug nuts that connect the wheel to the car."

Art begins to loosen the lug nuts. It's hard work. The car is old and the lug nuts are hard to move. As he works, some of the hospital patients come to the fence to watch him. They don't say anything, they just look.

"Oh, great! An audience of crazy people. Just what I need," Art complains.

He remembers that the next step is to jack up, or lift, the back of the car so he can get the wheel off. While he is doing that, it begins to rain. All the patients disappear into the mental hospital.

"Goodbye," says Art thankfully. "I don't like people watching me make a fool of myself."

He speaks too soon. One of the patients, a tiny old woman in a pink raincoat and a yellow rainhat, returns with a big, black umbrella. She holds onto the fence with one hand and silently watches what Art is doing.

Art pretends not to notice. He jacks up the car and finishes removing the lug nuts. He remembers his father teaching him, "Always put the lug nuts in the hub cap. That way, they can't be lost." Art carefully puts the four lug nuts in the hub cap. He carefully puts the hub cap next to the car. Then he goes to get the spare tire from the trunk. The old woman with the umbrella watches all this with great interest.

Suddenly a truck comes down the road. It is a big, wide truck and it is traveling fast. As it passes, its front left wheel hits Art's hub cap, kicks it into the corn field. The lug nuts go flying. The truck disappears. "This must be a bad dream!" Art cries. "This can't really be happening to me." Oh, but it is.

He searches up and down the rows of corn. All he gets for his trouble is wet. Finally he returns to his car. The lug nuts are gone. So is his chance of selling insurance to the farmer. So, he's quite sure, is his new job.

The old woman with the umbrella speaks up. "Hey, Mister, can't find those lug nuts, can you? Looks hopeless, doesn't it? May I give you some advice?"

Art doesn't answer. The last thing he wants is advice from a patient in a mental hospital. The old woman probably doesn't even know how to drive.

But the funny little woman goes right on talking.

"If you remove one lug nut from each of the other wheels," she says, "you're going to have three you can put on this one. There's a big town only a mile and a half down this road. With three lug nuts on each of your wheels, you can get there easily."

Art looks at the old woman with his mouth open. He can hardly believe that this strange little person in the pink raincoat and the yellow rainhat is going to rescue him. He takes her hand through the bars of the fence.

"Lady," he says, "I can never, never thank you enough." The rain is over. The old woman closes her black umbrella and starts to walk back to the hospital.

"You know," she says to Art over her shoulder, "I may be crazy but I'm not stupid."

EXERCISES

I. VOCABULARY

You probably know many of these words from reading the story and looking at the pictures. If there are still some you don't know, look them up in your dictionary now.

lonely	mental	salesman	rescue
lug nuts	middle	loosen	insurance
appointment	path	flat	patient
spare	smooth		

II. DEFINITIONS

Try to guess the best definition for these words. Then look them up in your dictionary and draw a circle around the answer.

1. mental   a. gold, silver, iron

   b. of or about the mind

   c. every month

2. smooth   a. not ready

   b. not rough

   c. not clean

3. spare   a. not needed until later

   b. necessary

   c. a kind of fruit

4. appointment   a. a place to live

   b. a time to meet someone

   c. something very sharp

5. flat   a. weigh too much

   b. fall

   c. without air

6. loosen   a. to make less tight

   b. to pay attention, to hear

   c. to fail to keep

III. READING COMPREHENSION

Read the questions. Find the answers in the story. Write the answers under the question.

1. With whom does Art have an appointment in Northern Kansas?

_____

_____

2. How does Art know he has a flat tire?

_____

_____

3. When you change a tire, you take off the hub cap or wheel cover first. What do you do next?

_____

_____

4. Which of the patients comes back with an unbrella to watch what Art is doing?

_____

_____

5. Why is Art glad when the mental patients go back to the hospital?

_____

_____

6. When the old woman offers Art advice, why doesn't he answer?

_____

_____

IV. DISCUSSION

Look at the pictures. Talk to your partner. Use words from the story.

Picture #1
Where does Art put the lug nuts that he takes off?
Why does he put them there?
What happens to the lug nuts?

Picture #2
What is Art looking for in the
corn field?
Does he find what he is looking for?
The story says that all he gets
for his trouble is wet. How
does that happen?

V. WRITING

Dictation. Study the first paragraph in the story for a few minutes. Think about spelling and punctuation. Then close your book and write as the teacher dictates. When you finish, open your book and check your work. Correct your mistakes.

_____

_____

_____

_____

_____

_____

Sweetie hates to go to the laundromat.

Sweetie's Washing Machine

Sharon Sweet needs one hundred and sixteen dollars. Her washing machine is broken. That's how much it costs to fix it. Sweetie — which is what everyone calls Sharon — really wants to repair that old machine. She hates to go to the laundromat. So she saves her money slowly, a little at a time. She puts the nickels and dimes and quarters in an empty coffee can.

Saving money is not easy. Sweetie's smile is brave and bright but her life is hard. She is a single mother who goes to school every day. She is learning how to use a computer. At night, she cleans offices in a big office building. She has to pay rent for her apartment. She has to pay the baby sitter who takes care of her daughter, Tanya. Sweetie gets a pay check on Friday. By Wednesday there is almost no money left.

Still, Sweetie makes up her mind to fix that washing machine somehow.

It's important because she wants to spend Sundays with Tanya. She wants to read to her and play with her in the park. She can't do that if she spends her only free day at the laundromat. When Sweetie makes up her mind to do something, she does it. Every cent she can possibly save goes into the coffee can. Even when Tanya asks for ice cream, Sweetie says no. "You know why," Sweetie reminds the child. "We need that washing machine. But you just wait. When Mama gets a good job in a big office we're going to buy everything we want. Almost."

"Then can I have that doll that looks like me?" Tanya asks.

There is a doll in a toy store window that Tanya wants very much. "Yes. Then you can. I promise," Sweetie says.

"After I get the doll, you can buy those earrings you like," Tanya tells her mother. "You're going to be so beautiful! If you wear those earrings, I'm sure a millionaire is going to fall in love with you."

Sweetie smiles. "Just a plain, ordinary millionaire? Why not a prince?"

Mother and daughter burst out laughing.

One day, Sweetie counts the money in the coffee can. There are almost sixty dollars. That day, Sweetie's younger sister Laura phones. Laura goes to high school. She has an invitation to a party. She wants to buy a new dress. Can Sweetie lend her thirty dollars?

"No. N, O," Sweetie says, "I'm sorry, I can't."

She asks herself how she feels about saying no to her sister. She finds that she feels all right about it.

When there are almost ninety dollars in the can, one of Sweetie's friends calls. He has a car payment to make. Can Sweetie lend him fifty dollars until Tuesday?

"I can't. I'm sorry," Sweetie tells him.

She asks herself how she feels about saying no to a friend. She feels a little bad, but not bad enough to change her mind.

Finally there are one hundred and sixteen dollars in the can. Sweetie takes Tanya by the hand.

"Let's go to the bank and get paper money," she says. "I don't want to pay the washing machine repair man with nickels and dimes and quarters."

Outside the apartment house, Sweetie and Tanya meet old Mrs. Bernstein. She is sitting in the sun, as usual. Her poor old dog, Harry, is lying on her knees, as usual. But Harry doesn't swing his tail when Tanya pets him. He doesn't even open his eyes.

"Mrs, Bernstein, I think Harry is sick," Sweetie says. "Aren't you going to take him to the animal hospital?"

The old woman looks at Sweetie sadly. "That costs a lot of money," she says. "And my government check isn't going to come for two weeks yet."

"I'm really sorry I can't help," Sweetie tells her. She and Tanya walk away. Sweetie asks herself how she feels about not helping Mrs. Bernstein. She feels very bad. She knows the dog is the old woman's only friend. She walks slower and slower. Then she turns back.

"Mrs. Bernstein, please take Harry to the animal hospital," Sweetie says. "It's all right. I can pay for it."

"Mama, why are you doing this?" Tanya asks when they are alone. "You know we have to fix the washing machine."

"I know," Sweetie says. "We're just going to have to fix it a few weeks later. Mrs. Bernstein is going to pay us back."

Tanya is unhappy. "Is that dog more important than the doll that looks like me? More important than the earrings? More important than the washing machine?"

"I think so," Sweetie answers. "Look, Baby, you and I have each other to love, but Mrs. Bernstein only has Harry. The doll and the earrings have to wait. The washing machine has to wait. Anyway, I'm beginning to like the laundromat. I meet interesting people there. Someday a prince may come in to wash his shirts and socks. The prince may see me and fall in love with me."

"A prince? In a laundromat?" Tanya asks.

Sweetie laughs. To her own surprise, she is feeling happy. "Why not?" she says.

EXERCISES

I. VOCABULARY

You probably know many of these words from reading the story and looking at the pictures. If there are still some you don't know, look them up in your dictionary now.

empty	count	save	cent
payment	brave	invitation	repair
rent	enough	daughter	plain
usual	somehow	ordinary	

II. DEFINITIONS

Try to guess the best definition for these words. Then look them up in your dictionary and draw a circle around the answer.

1. daughter
   - a. a boy
   - b. a girl
   - c. a dog

2. usual
   - a. happens once
   - b. never happens
   - c. happens most of the time

3. somehow
   - a. in one way or another
   - b. some person
   - c. some thing

4. empty
   - a. containing nothing
   - b. containing a little
   - c. containing much

5. cent
   - a. more than a dime
   - b. more than a nickel
   - c. less than a nickel

6. repair
   - a. a pair
   - b. to pay back
   - c. to fix

III. READING COMPREHENSION

Read the questions. Find the answers in the story. Write the answers under the questions.

1. Why is Sweetie putting money in an empty coffee can?

   _____

   _____

2. What does Sweetie want to do on Sunday?

   _____

   _____

3. Why does Sweetie's sister want to borrow thirty dollars?

   _____

   _____

4. What kind of smile does Sweetie have?

   _____

   _____

5. What is Sweetie going to get at the bank? Why?

   _____

   _____

6. How does Sweetie know that Mrs. Bernstein's dog is sick?

   _____

   _____

IV. DISCUSSION

Look at the pictures. Talk to your partner. Use words from the story.

Picture #1
Where is Tanya?
Which doll does she want? Why?
When is she going to get that doll?

Picture #2
Where is Mrs. Bernstein sitting?
Where is Harry?
Where does Sweetie think Harry ought to go?
How does Sweetie feel about not helping Mrs. Bernstein?

V. WRITING

Dictation. Study the first paragraph in the story. Think about spelling and punctuation. Then close your book and write as the teacher dictates. When you finish, open your book and check your work. Correct your mistakes.

_____

_____

_____

_____

_____

_____

The taxi driver leans out of the window. "There's room for one more," he says gently.

There Is Room For One More

Norah Nelson is a lucky woman and she knows it. Her problems usually have happy endings and most of her dreams come true. At age thirty-four she owns a successful business in Chicago. She has a loving husband and two dear children. Happy and healthy, Norah lives her life with confidence. She has no reason to be afraid of anything until...until one day...

One day, Norah has to fly to a business meeting in New York. Whenever she goes there, she stays at least one night with her sister Ellen and her brother-in-law Greg. Their home is not really in the big city, but close. In the morning, Norah always rides to New York with Greg who works there.

The sisters enjoy each other and talk for hours. It is late by the time Norah goes upstairs to sleep. She falls asleep right away but wakes up at one-thirty without knowing why. Maybe she is cold, she thinks. She gets out of bed to close the window. The moon is full. The driveway that leads to the house looks silver in the moonlight. As Norah watches, a black station wagon comes slowly up the driveway.

"Who can be arriving at this hour?" Norah wonders. The station wagon gets closer and stops under her window. Now she can see that there are four or five passengers. The left front door opens and the driver gets out. Norah looks at his face and feels as if an ice-cold finger is touching her heart. It is the face of someone who is dead...dead and buried a long, long time. The driver holds the station wagon door open. He looks directly up at Norah.

"There is room for one more," he says gently.

Without even thinking, Norah closes the window as fast and as hard as she can. Her heart is racing wildly. "What I am seeing is impossible," Norah thinks. "Maybe I'm dreaming and don't know it. Yes, I am certainly dreaming."

Though she is still afraid, she is also curious. She lifts the curtain a tiny bit and looks. There is nothing but moonlight on the driveway.

Norah doesn't sleep the rest of the night. At breakfast, she tells her sister and brother-in-law about her dream.

"I suppose it's a dream," she says. "What else can it be?"

"Just a very bad dream," Ellen agrees. Greg thinks so too. He reminds Norah that he has an early appointment in New York. "We have to hurry, so kiss Ellen goodbye," he says.

The drive to the city is good for Norah. She begins to feel better. After all, anyone can have a bad dream. When they are near the bank where Greg works she tells him to let her out.

"You don't have to drive me to my meeting," she says. "I'm going to take a taxi the rest of the way."

Finding a taxi in New York is not easy. Two or three go by, but they are occupied. Finally one stops. Norah opens the door. She is about to step in when she sees that there already are two passengers. The taxi driver leans out of the window. Norah recognizes the driver of the station wagon. His dead face smiles at her. "There is room for one more," he says gently.

Norah screams and backs away from the taxi. She runs, not knowing, not caring where she is going. She almost knocks over an old man. She tries to say "I'm sorry," but no words come out of her mouth. She sees steps leading to a subway station. She runs down, gets on the first train that comes. The train is almost full. Norah looks at everyone carefully. They are just ordinary people like herself. Being among them makes her feel better. She knows that she must get to her meeting soon. She leaves the subway at the next station and walks the rest of the way.

The meeting is in the Franklin Building on West 47th Street. Norah takes the elevator to the nineteenth floor. The secretary says, "They're waiting for you, Ms. Nelson. Do you want a glass of water? You look so pale."

"I'm fine, thanks," Norah says, and joins the other business people at the meeting. It is hard for her to pay attention to the speakers. She keeps remembering the strange things that are happening to her. Is it possible to dream while you are wide awake? Norah decides to see her doctor as soon as she can. She makes an excuse to leave the meeting early. "I have to fly to Chicago this evening," she explains.

In the hall she waits for an elevator that is going down. At last one stops on the nineteenth floor. The doors open. The elevator is crowded but the elevator operator smiles and says gently, "There is room for one more."

Norah takes one look at that terrible, that familiar dead face and runs. She finds the stairs. She slips and breaks the high heel of her shoe but she keeps running. She has only one thought, to get away from here, and she pays no attention to anything else. There is a distant sound, like thunder, and the tall building shakes a little. Norah doesn't notice. There are other people going down the stairs. She doesn't notice. All she cares about is running. Down, down all nineteen floors she goes and at last reaches the street exit. Outside, hundreds of people are standing around. Ambulances and police cars are arriving. A man near Norah says, "What a terrible thing! Nobody expects an elevator to fall and kill every passenger."

Finally Norah is paying attention. "From what floor?" she whispers.

"Everybody says the nineteenth floor," the man tells her.

EXERCISES

I. VOCABULARY

You probably know many of these words from reading the story and looking at the pictures. If there are still some you don't know, look them up in your dictionary now.

curious	reasonable	occupied	operator
racing	confidence	excuse	ordinary
appointment	attention	passenger	familiar
enjoy	recognize	problem	

II. DEFINITIONS

Try to guess the best definition for these words. Then look them up in your dictionary and draw a circle around the answer.

1. ordinary
   a. a hospital worker
   b. a command
   c. usual or average

2. curious
   a. very angry
   b. to want to know something
   c. to cure an illness

3. attention
   a. the act of speaking
   b. the act of listening
   c. the act of moving

4. problem
   a. something that is simple
   b. something that is lost
   c. something that is difficult

5. enjoy
   a. experience with pleasure
   b. experience with fear
   c. experience with pain

6. passenger
   a. a student who gets good grades
   b. a dangerous driver
   c. someone who travels in a car, ship, train, or plane

III. READING COMPREHENSION

Read the questions. Find the answers in the story. Write the answers under the question.

1. What can Norah Nelson see when the station wagon stops under her window?

_____

_____

2. What does she see the second time she looks out of the window?

_____

_____

3. How does Norah feel when her brother-in-law gives her a ride to the city?

_____

_____

4. Why does being with the other passengers in the subway train make Norah feel better?

_____

_____

5. Why is it hard for Norah to pay attention to the speakers at the meeting?

_____

_____

6. What does Norah see when she finally leaves the building?

_____

_____

IV. DISCUSSION

Look at the pictures. Talk to your partner. Use words from the story.

Picture #1
When she first sees the station wagon, what does Norah wonder?
What is it about the driver that frightens her so much?
What does he say to her?
What does she do?

Picture #2
What excuse does Norah give for leaving the meeting early?
Why is she waiting in the hall?
After she sees the face of the elevator operator, what does she do?

V. WRITING

The story says that Norah is a lucky woman. List four ways in which she is lucky.

1. _____

2. _____

3. _____

4. _____

His dark glasses hide his eyes so it is hard to know what he is thinking.

Mrs. Wright and Mr. Wrong

In our town there is a woman who is always right. Even her name is right, Mrs. Josephine Wright. Her husband's name is Albert Wright, but he is often wrong. If Albert Wright says it looks like rain, his wife says it does not. She is right. The clouds blow away and the sun comes out. But when Mrs. Wright says it looks like rain, it rains so hard all the streets flood.

Mr. Wright thinks the New York Yankees are going to win the baseball game. Mrs. Wright says, "No, Albert, I am certain they are going to lose."

"But Josephine," Mr. Wright argues, "you don't know anything about baseball. You're not even interested in baseball."

He is wasting his time. The Yankees lose, 9 to 1.

Mrs. Wright is not only always right, she also knows everything. If Mr. Wright buys a shirt, Mrs. Wright knows a store where the same shirt is two dollars cheaper. When the neighbor hangs out her wash, Mrs. Wright goes over there right away. She tells the neighbor what she can do to make her sheets whiter. When her sister-in-law Sally buys a new green dress, Mrs. Wright explains to Sally why green is not a good color for her.

Sally is Albert's sister. Albert tells his wife he thinks Sally's feelings are hurt about the dress.

"Oh, you're wrong again, Albert," insists Mrs. Wright. "She knows I'm just trying to help her."

Sally's daughter Martha is getting married. Josephine and Albert receive an invitation to the wedding.

"I like Martha," Mrs. Wright says. "I want to send a nice wedding present. We can buy them a table with a sun umbrella for their garden."

"They don't have a garden," her husband reminds her. "They're moving into a little apartment."

"That doesn't matter," answers Mrs. Wright. "They can put the present away until they do have a garden."

On the day of the wedding, Josephine Wright takes a long time to get dressed.

"We're going to be late for the wedding," Mr. Wright worries as they get into the car.

"No, we are not," says his wife. "I know a short cut. It's better than the freeway. Turn right at the next corner."

"That's not a short cut," Mr. Wright starts to say, but Mrs. Wright doesn't let him finish.

"Don't argue with me, Albert. You know I'm always right."

Because they are so late, Albert drives faster than usual. "Don't drive so fast," his wife says. "You're going to get a ticket."

Mrs. Wright is right again. Albert looks in his car mirror and sees a police officer on a motorcycle close behind him. The policeman motions Albert to pull over. He asks to see Albert's driver's license. Then he takes out his ticket book.

"Sir, do you know what the speed limit is?" the policeman asks.

Before Albert can answer, Mrs. Wright begins to talk. Her face is as pink as her hat because she is very angry.

"Officer," she says loudly, "I tell him over and over again that he drives too fast. But does he listen to me? Never. He does everything wrong. Because of him we're going to be late to a very important wedding. I know the name on his driver's license says Albert Wright, but it ought to say Albert Wrong."

The motorcycle policeman is very tall. His high black boots shine. His wide black belt shines. His dark glasses shine. He looks at Mrs. Wright silently. The dark glasses hide his eyes so it is hard to know what he is thinking. After a while he hands the license back to Mr. Wright.

"Thank you, sir," he says. "Drive carefully and have a nice day."

The policeman puts away his book. He gets on his motorcycle.

Mrs. Wright sticks her head in its pink hat out of the car window. "Officer, aren't you going to give my husband a ticket?" she asks.

"No, he has enough trouble already," the policeman answers. **Vroom**... **vroom**... **vroom!** He speeds away.

"Albert, what does he mean when he says you have enough trouble already?" Mrs. Wright wants to know.

Mr. Wright smiles to himself. "I have no idea," he says.

EXERCISES

I. VOCABULARY

You probably know many of these words from reading the story and looking at the pictures. If there are still some you don't know, look them up in your dictionary now.

flood	certain	remind	sister-in-law
matter	cheaper	worries	finish
short cut	argue	neighbor	freeway
wasting	invitation	explain	

II. DEFINITIONS

Try to guess the best definition for these words. Then look them up in your dictionary and draw a circle around the answer.

1. cheaper
   a. costs more money
   b. costs less money
   c. it is free

2. neighbor
   a. lives near you
   b. lives in the same city
   c. lives in the same country

3. finish
   a. born in Finland
   b. begin something
   c. complete something

4. sister-in-law
   a. my father's sister
   b. my brother's sister
   c. my wife's sister

5. remind
   a. remember
   b. obey
   c. cause someone to remember

6. argue
   a. give reasons for or against
   b. agree
   c. quarrel

III. READING COMPREHENSION

Read the questions. Find the answers in the story. Write the answers under the questions.

1. Who is Sally?

_____

_____

2. What happens when Albert Wright says it looks like rain?

_____

_____

3. What does Josephine Wright do on the day of the wedding?

_____

_____

4. Why does Albert drive faster than usual?

_____

_____

5. What does the motorcycle policeman ask to see?

_____

_____

6. What is the police officer's reason for not giving Albert a ticket?

_____

_____

IV. DISCUSSION

Look at the pictures. Talk to your partner.
Use words from the story.

Picture #1
Why does Mrs. Wright go to her neighbor's
house?
Do you think she is helping her neighbor?
Do you think the neighbor likes to be told
that her sheets are not white
enough?

Picture #2
Why is Mrs. Wright so angry?
Does she want her husband to
get a ticket?
Why do you think so?

V. WRITING

Write four sentences that describe the motorcycle policeman.

1. _____

_____

2. _____

_____

3. _____

_____

4. _____

_____

47

Galileo is not on trial because of anything he does, but because of what he thinks.

The Trial of Galileo

The year is 1633. The trial of Galileo Galilei, in Rome, is an important event in world history. Galileo is not on trial because of what he does, but because of what he thinks. He disagrees with a belief of the Catholic Church. At that time, all real power belongs to the Church. It controls not only religion but science, the universities, and every-day life as well. No one questions the beliefs of the Church because that can be dangerous. Galileo's punishment is prison for the rest of his life. He is one of the greatest scientists of all time. Why is this happening to him?

The scientific belief of that period is that the earth is the center of the universe and does not move. The sun, moon, stars and planets revolve, or circle, around it. This belief is accepted as fact for more than a thousand years. In 1493, Copernicus, a Polish astronomer, writes a book in which he argues that the sun, not the earth, is the center of a great, complicated astronomical system. The moon and the planets, which include the earth, revolve around the sun. Copernicus dies just as his book is printed, so he escapes the anger of the Catholic Church.

As a young man, Galileo teaches mathematics and physics at the University of Pisa. He begins to question certain beliefs when he sees that professors continue to teach ancient science as fact even when it is not true. One of these beliefs is that heavy objects fall faster than light ones. One day, as students laugh and applaud, Galileo climbs to the top of the Leaning Tower of Pisa. He drops various balls, some heavy, some light — and proves they all fall at the same speed. After that, many professors suddenly do not like Galileo.

He moves on to the University of Padua. There he meets another scientist, Giordano Bruno. The Church orders the arrest of Bruno because he thinks Copernicus is right and says so. After eight years of prison and torture he still refuses to change his opinion. One night churchmen wearing hoods over their heads take Bruno out of his cell and burn him to death.

Whatever new thoughts Galileo now has about Copernicus he keeps to himself. He is becoming well known for his invention of the thermometer and for other scientific work. But in 1609 something happens to make him an astronomer. An eyeglass maker in Holland puts two different lenses inside a small wooden tube. When someone looks through the tube, distant objects seem four or five times closer. Men sell this tube on the streets of big cities, like a toy. Galileo quickly realizes how important this toy can be. In one day, he builds the world's first telescope. In a few years, he increases its power four hundred times. It is the beginning of a new astronomy, a new age of science.

Every night Galileo studies the sky with his telescope. He discovers four of the moons of Jupiter. (We now know there are eleven.) He observes that the moons revolve around Jupiter while Jupiter itself rotates, or turns. Isn't this the same as the earth and its moon? Copernicus is right, the earth moves.

His discovery of Jupiter's moons makes Galileo the hero of Europe. Poets write poems about him. People call him the Columbus of the heavens. But the Church is not happy, especially after Galileo suggests that our universe may be only one of many. In 1616, Pope Paul V, the religious leader of the Catholic Church, orders Galileo to come to Rome. There he is warned that he must not believe or teach the ideas of Copernicus. Remembering Giordano Bruno, Galileo agrees to obey.

In 1623, Pope Paul V dies. Galileo hopes the new Pope, Urban VIII, is going to permit him to think and work freely. He is wrong. In 1633, Galileo again receives an order to come to to Rome. By this time, he is old, sick and walking with difficulty. The church leaders who question him make it clear that, unless he admits he is guilty, he must face torture. Galileo falls to his knees and tells his judges anything they want to hear. Yes, yes, yes, he no longer believes Copernicus is right. There is a story that, as he rises from his knees, Galileo whispers, "E pur si muove." In Italian that means, "But it does move!" He is, of course, referring to the earth and its movement around the sun. Is this story true? We don't know. Many people like to think so.

Galileo's punishment is prison for the rest of his life. But he has powerful friends who arrange for him to be imprisoned in his own home. He slowly becomes blind and dies in 1641.

But that is not the end of the trial of Galileo. For centuries, the Galileo case continues to trouble the Catholic Church. In 1979, Pope John Paul II appoints a committee to study the whole matter. Thirteen years later, the committee returns to the Vatican with their report. They tell the television cameras and the world that the mistakes of the Church against Galileo must be honestly admitted. It is an apology.

The next day, the headline in the New York Times reads: "AFTER 350 YEARS CATHOLIC CHURCH SAYS GALILEO IS RIGHT: IT MOVES."

The headline in La Repubblica, a national newspaper in Italy, says: GALILEO, EXCUSE ME. And below are the words, "E pur si muove."

EXERCISES

I. VOCABULARY

You probably know many of these words from reading the story and looking at the pictures. If there are still some you don't know, look them up in your dictionary now.

event	various	applaud	trial
complicated	punishment	universe	century
proves	lens	astronomy	thermometer
apology	obey	revolve	

II. DEFINITIONS

Try to guess the best definition for these words. Then look them up in your dictionary and draw a circle around the answer.

1. apology
   a. an expression of regret
   b. an expression of anger
   c. an expression on one's face

2. century
   a. ten years
   b. one hundred years
   c. one thousand years

3. revolve
   a. shoot
   b. turn around
   c. become

4. complicated
   a. opposite of clean
   b. opposite of soft
   c. opposite of simple

5. event
   a. an opening to let in air
   b. something important that happens
   c. something that happens in the evening

6. trial
   a. an examination before judges
   b. something in three parts
   c. a path through a forest

III. READING COMPREHENSION

Read the questions. Find the answers in the story. Write the answers under the questions.

1. Why is Galileo on trial?

_____

_____

2. What does Galileo prove when he drops heavy and light balls at the same time from the Leaning Tower of Pisa?

_____

_____

3. What does Copernicus believe?

_____

_____

4. What does Galileo suggest about our universe?

_____

_____

5. What does the Church warn Galileo not to do?

_____

_____

6. What does the Catholic Church tell the world in 1992?

_____

_____

IV. DISCUSSION

Look at the pictures. Talk to your partner. Use words from the story.

Picture # 1
What old scientific beliefs are some professors still teaching?
What does Galileo prove when he climbs to the top of the Leaning Tower of Pisa?
How does he do that?

Picture #2
How does Galileo get the idea of building the world's first telescope?
What does Galileo learn from observing the moons of Jupiter?

V. WRITING

What is the belief of the Catholic Church that Copernicus argues is not true? List the three parts of that belief.

1. _____

2. _____

3. _____

The people in the street look at each other. They are afraid to say anything.
Suddenly a little girl pulls at her mother's skirt.

The Emperor's New Clothes
A play
Adapted from a story by Hans Christian Andersen

THE CHARACTERS:	The Emperor
	Hans and Erik
	First and Second Ministers
	Servants, merchants, soldiers, people
	A little girl

<u>**SCENE 1:**</u>	*The Emperor's private apartment in the palace. It doesn't seem very private. There are at least fifty people in the room. A barber is cutting the Emperor's hair in the latest style. A shoemaker is selling him new shoes. A tailor holds up yellow and purple suits for the Emperor to admire. Almost everyone has something to sell to the Emperor. Everyone except Hans and Erik. They stand at the back of the crowd, quietly watching.*
HANS:	*(whispers)* Erik, can you guess what I am thinking?
ERIK:	*(whispers back)* I don't have to guess. I already know. Our Emperor is a dressed-up monkey who buys anything.
HANS:	Please don't call the Emperor a monkey. Show some respect. I like him. I have a feeling he is going to make us rich.
	(Hans and Erik put their heads together and talk in low voices. When they are finished, they smile at each other. They move close to the Emperor.)
ERIK:	*(coughs to get the Emperor's attention)* Oh, great Emperor, my brother and I are weavers. We make thread into cloth. We travel all the way to China to buy silk thread. Ours is the finest cloth anyone can buy.

HANS:	*(pretends to be impatient)* Erik, don't waste the Emperor's precious time. Yes, our cloth is very fine, but that is not important.
ERIK:	Well then, we weave the most <u>beautiful</u> cloth in the world.
HANS:	Erik, be quiet. Beautiful is not important.
EMPEROR:	*(interested)* If fine is not important, and beautiful is not important, what <u>is</u> important?
HANS:	Oh, great Emperor, clothes made out of our cloth are sometimes invisible. I don't know why. I am just a simple fellow. Only very stupid people are not able to see our cloth. Everyone else can. It is a mystery.
EMPEROR:	What a wonderful mystery! I must have a suit made out of your cloth. Then I can finally know which of my ministers is wise and which is a fool. First Minister, give these brothers a hundred pieces of gold to buy silk thread. Second Minister, get them looms upon which to weave their cloth. I want my new suit as soon as possible. Or even sooner.
SCENE 2:	*A room in which there are two looms with absolutely no weaving on them. Hans and Erik are playing cards. There is a knock at the door. They put away the cards. Each brother sits at a loom, pretending to weave. The First Minister enters. The empty looms make him nervous.*
FIRST MINISTER:	Excuse me. I don't want to interrupt. I just want to see... *(he clears his throat)*... yes, to see how the weaving is coming...is coming along.
ERIK:	Ah, I understand. And do you, in fact...see?
HANS:	Erik, of course he sees! The First Minister is not stupid.

FIRST MINISTER:	No... certainly not... the cloth is beautiful, beautiful. I must hurry to report to the Emperor. Good day to you both.
ERIK:	Remind the Emperor we need more gold to buy more silk.
FIRST MINISTER:	Yes, yes, I promise to tell him immediately.
SCENE 3:	*The same room, a few weeks later. The looms are still empty. The brothers are eating chicken and apple cake. They have no time to hide the food because the Emperor walks in without knocking.*
EMPEROR:	Everyone tells me the cloth is finished. They say it is beautiful. I am here to see for myself.
HANS:	*(pretends to hold a long piece of cloth over his arm)* It is an honor to show our work to our great Emperor.
EMPEROR:	*(can't talk for a moment, when he does, his voice shakes)* I want to be alone with this...this cloth. *(Hans and Erik leave. The Emperor speaks to himself.)* What terrible trouble I am in! I can't see the cloth. To me it looks like nothing, like air. That proves that I am stupid. If I am stupid, how can I be the Emperor? Oh dear, oh dear, no one must ever find out. *(He calls.)* First Minister, come at once! *(First Minister hurries in.)* Tell my tailor to make me a suit out of this beautiful cloth. I want it by Christmas.
SCENE 4:	*A public street. Crowds of people are waiting. Everybody knows the Emperor is going to ride by on his way to church. Everybody knows he is wearing his famous new clothes. And here he comes now, on his white horse, surrounded by his servants and soldiers and ministers.*

SECOND MINISTER: *(to First Minister)* The Emperor's new clothes fit him well, don't they?

FIRST MINISTER: Oh, yes. Perfectly. A perfect fit.

(The people in the street look at each other. They are afraid to say anything. Suddenly a little girl pulls at her mother's skirt.)

LITTLE GIRL: *(in a high, clear voice)* Mommy, the Emperor isn't wearing any clothes! He's out in the street in his underwear!

(The laughter begins with the people close to the little girl. It spreads and spreads until everyone is laughing. Hans and Erik are, as usual, standing at the back of the crowd.)

ERIK: Brother, can you guess what I'm thinking?

HANS: I don't have to guess. I already know. It's time to take our bags of gold and quietly disappear. *(And they do.)*

EXERCISES

I. VOCABULARY

You probably know many of these words from reading the story and looking at the pictures. If there are still some you don't know, look them up in your dictionary now.

minister	admire	mystery	surround
impatient	private	weave	thread
prove	cloth	merchant	invisible
pretend	skirt	loom	

II. DEFINITIONS

Try to guess the best definition for these words. Then look them up in your dictionary and draw a circle around the answer.

1. invisible
   a. can be seen
   b. can not be seen
   c. can not be heard

2. mystery
   a. easy to understand
   b. a record of the past
   c. hard to understand

3. weave
   a. to make cloth
   b. to go away
   c. a movement of the ocean

4. admire
   a. disappear
   b. dislike
   c. like

5. respect
   a. honor
   b. expect
   c. remind

6. merchant
   a. sails a boat
   b. sells something
   c. tells something

III. Reading Comprehension

Read the questions. Find the answers in the story. Write the answers under the questions.

1. At the beginning of the play, what is the barber doing?

_____

_____

2. What does Hans say to explain why he likes the Emperor?

_____

_____

3. Why does the Emperor want a suit made out of cloth that stupid people can't see?

_____

_____

4. What does Hans do when the Emperor comes to see the cloth for himself?

_____

_____

5. What does the cloth look like to the Emperor?

_____

_____

6. What does the little girl say?

_____

_____

IV. DISCUSSION

Look at the pictures. Talk to your partner. Use words from the story.

Picture #1:
Where is the Emperor while he is getting his hair cut?
Do you think the Emperor likes clothes? Give reasons for your opinion. What are Hans and Erik doing while the Emperor is getting a haircut?

Picture #2:
What are Hans and Erik doing?
Does the First Minister really see cloth on the looms?
What does the First Minister say about the cloth?
Why is he afraid to tell the truth?

V. WRITING

In Scene One we read that there are at least fifty people in the Emperor's private apartment. Name six people who are there.

1. _____ 2. _____

3. _____ 4. _____

5. _____ 6. _____

Yellow Bird walks seven days, through dark forests and across running rivers. At last she comes to the tipi she sees every night in her dreams.

Yellow Bird and the Seven Brothers
(A Legend of the Cheyenne Indian People)

Long, long ago, when the world is almost new . . .

. . . a young girl lives with her parents in a Cheyenne village in North America. The girl's name is Yellow Bird because she is small and pretty, like a bird. She is an only child and a joy to her parents. Everyone in the village is proud of her and of her beautiful embroidery, or sewing. Each buffalo blanket she makes has bright, wonderful colors. Each one is embroidered with unusual patterns of beads and feathers. No one can embroider like Yellow Bird.

One day, Yellow Bird's mother notices that her daughter is sewing a man's shirt. She is making it out of the finest, softest white deerskin. She is embroidering it with rare beads and feathers. The mother wonders for whom Yellow Bird is making this shirt. Her father already owns one, and she has no brothers.

"Is this shirt for a young man you wish to marry?" the mother asks.

"No," says Yellow Bird, "I don't know any young man I wish to marry."

"For whom, then?" the mother inquires.

Yellow Bird answers, "I don't know yet. I only know this is something I need to do."

Many weeks pass. Yellow Bird finishes the shirt and immediately begins work on another. She makes six, all alike. When the sixth shirt is finished, her mother again questions her.

"My daughter, do you know yet for whom you are making these shirts?"

"I think I am beginning to know," Yellow Bird replies. She starts to work on a seventh shirt. This one is smaller than the others. It is a shirt for a young boy. When it is finished, Yellow Bird tells her mother, "In my dreams I see seven brothers. They are far away from here but they are waiting for me to be their sister. I must go to them."

Yellow Bird packs the seven shirts and her own clothes. Her mother and father help her and walk with her part of the way.

"Do you know where to go?" the father asks.

Yellow Bird says, "I think so." Then the three of them say a loving goodbye. Yellow Bird continues her journey. She walks seven days, through dark forests and across running rivers. At last she comes to the tipi she sees every night in her dreams. A young boy sits beside the tipi. He is waiting for her. He jumps to his feet to welcome her.

"My name is Five Arrows," he says. "I am the little brother. I send you dreams every night."

"I dream your dreams," Yellow Bird tells him, "and now I am here."

The little brother is happy with the beautiful shirt Yellow Bird gives him. The six older brothers now return from hunting buffalo. They are pleased with their shirts, too. They want Yellow Bird to be their sister. She wants all seven of them to be her brothers. They agree to live together.

One day, a buffalo calf comes to the tipi. "I come from the buffalo nation," he says. "We want Yellow Bird to be **our** sister. She must come with me."

"You can't have her," replies Five Arrows. "Go away!"

"Tomorrow, somebody bigger is going to come!" the calf promises.

The next day, a buffalo cow appears at the tipi. "I come from the buffalo nation," she says. "We want Yellow Bird. We want her now."

"You can **never** have her," Five Arrows replies. "Go away!"

"Tomorrow somebody bigger is going to come," the cow promises.

The next day, the six older brothers do not go hunting. They stay with Yellow Bird because she is afraid. Suddenly they hear what sounds like thunder. The entire buffalo nation surrounds the tipi. Their leader is the biggest buffalo in the world. His terrible eyes are blood red.

"Give us the girl," the great buffalo demands, "or I am going to kill you all!"

The whole buffalo nation begins to stamp on the ground. The ground shakes. Rocks fall from the mountains and rivers spill out of their beds. Five Arrows tells his sister and brothers to climb a tall tree nearby.

"Quickly! As fast as you can!" he cries. He takes out one of the five arrows he carries. With his bow he shoots it into the trunk of the tree. Then he himself jumps into one of the lower branches — and not a moment too soon. His arrow, which has great and special power, causes the tree to grow a thousand feet in less then a second. Way down below, the angry buffalo begins to attack the tree with his horns. Three times more the little brother shoots arrows into the tree. Three times more the tree grows taller and taller. But on the ground the great buffalo begins to cut through the tree trunk with his horns. At any moment the tree is going to fall.

"Use your last arrow, little brother," one of the elder brothers cries to him. "Use it now!"

Just as Five Arrows does so, the tree, still growing taller, begins to fall. But Yellow Bird and her seven brothers are able to step off into the clouds. They are safe in the sky. They are there still. On any clear night you can look up and see them. The seven brothers are the constellation, or group of stars, called Ursa Major. The white man's name for it is The Big Dipper. Not very far from them is Yellow Bird. She is the North Star, shining down on the earth forever.

EXERCISES

I. VOCABULARY

You probably know many of these words from reading the story and looking at the pictures. If there are still some you don't know, look them up in your dictionary now.

only	alike	entire	arrow
spill	pattern	tipi	trunk
buffalo	parents	rare	calf
embroider	surround	feather	

II. DEFINITIONS

Try to guess the best definition for these words. Then look them up in your dictionary and draw a circle around the answer.

1. spill
   a. know or write the letters of a word
   b. hurt or damage
   c. run or fall from a container

2. trunk
   a. a branch of a tree
   b. the main stem of a tree
   c. the roots of a tree

3. alike
   a. the same
   b. to love or like
   c. a body of water

4. entire
   a. part of a wheel
   b. whole or complete
   c. to come in

5. feather
   a. a man who is a parent
   b. a greater distance
   c. grows on a bird

6. buffalo
   a. a large animal
   b. to polish something
   c. a city

III. READING COMPREHENSION

Read the questions. Find the answers in the story. Write the answers under the questions.

1. Describe the buffalo blankets that Yellow Bird makes.

_____

_____

2. What is different about the seventh shirt that Yellow Bird makes?

_____

_____

3. After walking seven days, where does Yellow Bird come?

_____

_____

4. Who is the leader of the buffalo nation?

_____

_____

5. What is the special power of the arrows that Five Arrows shoots into the tree?

_____

_____

6. What are Yellow Bird and her brothers able to do just as the tree falls?

_____

_____

IV. DISCUSSION

Look at the pictures. Talk to your partner.Use words from the story.

Picture #1
Why does Five Arrows jump into one of the lower branches of the tree?
What is the buffalo leader doing?
Why is he doing that?
How many arrows does the little brother shoot into the tree?

Picture #2
What happens to the seven brothers after they reach the sky?
What happens to Yellow Bird?
What is the white man's name for the constellation Ursa Major?

V. WRITING

Dictation. Find the paragraph on the first page of the story which begins with the words, **"Many weeks pass . . . "** Study it, paying attention to spelling and punctuation. Then close your book and write as the teacher dictates. When you finish, open your book and check your work. Correct your mistakes.

_____

_____

_____

_____

_____

_____

_____

Near the market, Mrs. Winter sees a little boy with a carton.

Sunshine, Moonshine, and Mrs. Winter

Dr. John Kim looks serious. "Mrs. Winter," he says to the patient in his office, "your blood pressure is high again. Do you take your medicine?"

Mrs. Winter is his old school teacher. She is closer to seventy than she is to sixty, but she is still quite pretty and very sure of herself.

"Of course I do," she says. "Johnny, I think my blood pressure is up because I don't sleep well." She always calls Dr. Kim by his first name. She remembers him as an eight-year-old in her third grade class. She remembers a bright boy from South Korea, not yet able to speak a word of English but already good in science and the best catcher on the baseball team.

"You're alone too much," the doctor tells her. He likes her and worries about her. She's a widow. Her only daughter lives in England. "I'm just reading in a medical magazine that owning a pet often improves the health of older people. Why don't you get a dog?"

Mrs. Winter shakes her head. "I don't like dogs. They bark."

"Get a cat, then. Cats don't bark."

"Cats scratch the furniture," Mrs. Winter says.

"I have a dog that barks and a cat that scratches the furniture," Dr. Kim replies, "and I love them both. At least think about getting a pet. You need something new and interesting in your life."

Driving home, Mrs. Winter thinks about Dr. Kim's advice. Then she puts it out of her mind. Sometimes Johnny thinks he knows everything. No pet, thanks.

That night, as always, Mrs. Winter reads in bed for hours. She just can't sleep. In the morning, feeling very tired, she goes to the market. Near the door she sees a little boy with a carton and a sign that says: FREE KITTENS TO GOOD HOMES. The child looks at Mrs. Winter with hope in his eyes.

"There are only two left," he tells her. He picks up a tiny yellow kitten. "This one is Sunshine. The little black one is her brother. His name is Moonshine. They're good little kittens. Very clean."

"I'm sure they are," says Mrs. Winter, and walks into the market. As she shops for food, she again remembers Dr. Kim's advice. She wonders if a pet can really improve a person's health. On her way out she stops and looks in the carton again. The little yellow kitten is very sweet. She asks the boy, "What do they use to — you know, go to the bathroom?"

The boy tells her they use a box, with some sand in it. Mrs. Winter takes a deep breath. "I'll take the yellow one," she says, "Sunshine."

"Oh, please take both," the boy begs. "They are going to be so lonesome!"

"One is enough," Mrs. Winter says. "Probably more than enough."

At home, Mrs. Winter puts Sunshine down on the living room floor. At first the kitten just sits there, examining everything with her perfectly round green eyes. Then she goes off in every direction. On top of the bookcase. Under the bed. Inside the broom closet. When night comes, Mrs. Winter is so tired from running after Sunshine that she can hardly keep her eyes open.

"I am sure to sleep tonight," she thinks. She puts Sunshine in the bathroom with food, water and her box. Then she closes the bathroom door and gets into bed. Immediately, the kitten starts scratching at the door and crying. She does it most of the night and Mrs. Winter hardly sleeps at all.

"It's because she's so lonesome for her brother," Mrs. Winter decides. "It's really wrong of me to separate them. Oh, dear, suppose the little boy isn't at the market today? Suppose Moonshine belongs to someone else already?" But the boy is there, and so is Moonshine. Mrs. Winter takes the black kitten home. Sunshine is so happy to see him! The two of them roll around like little balls of fur. They are everywhere. Mrs. Winter, enjoying herself, has an imaginary talk with her doctor. "Johnny," she says, "is this what you mean by something new and interesting in my life?"

That evening, Mrs. Winter is even more tired than the night before. At eight o'clock she tells the kittens, "It's bedtime." She puts them in the bathroom with food, water and their box and closes the door. Then she gets into bed and turns off the light. As soon as she does, the kittens begin to cry and scratch at the door. Both of them.

Mrs. Winter is getting angry. She opens the bathroom door and shakes her finger at the kittens. "You are very bad," she tells them. "You are not lonesome for each other anymore. So what is the matter with you now?"

Both kittens run to Mrs. Winter's bed and climb up. Quite happy on the blanket, they are busy washing themselves and each other. Mrs. Winter begins to understand. They think she is their mother. They want to sleep with her.

"No, no," Mrs. Winter says, "that's not the way it's going to be! Just tonight, because I'm too tired to do anything about it. But never again."

Moonshine lies on Mrs. Winter's stomach. Sunshine leans on her shoulder. Both kittens seem to have tiny motors inside of them that go purrrrrr, purrrrrr, purrrrrr. It's a very pleasant sound. Listening, Mrs. Winter's eyes close. The next thing she knows it is nine o'clock. Nine o'clock in the morning! Mrs. Winter can hardly believe it. She feels wonderful. "Thanks, you good little kittens," she says. "Do you want tuna fish for breakfast?"

In a few weeks it is time for Mrs. Winter to go to Dr. Kim's office again. He takes her blood pressure and gives her the good news.

"It's way down," he says. "Are you doing something new or different?"

She wonders, should she tell him that she sleeps with two kittens every night? Not yet. He's such a know-it-all, let him wait.

"Oh," she says mysteriously, "I'm just enjoying some Sunshine. Some Moonshine, too." And she gives the doctor her very nicest smile.

EXERCISES

I. VOCABULARY

You probably know many of these words from reading the story and looking at the pictures. If there are still some you don't know, look them up in your dictionary now.

pressure	health	improve	scratch
able	owning	breath	carton
blanket	separate	stomach	widow
enjoy	serious	lonesome	

II. DEFINITIONS

Try to guess the best definition for these words. Then look them up in your dictionary and draw a circle around the answer.

1. widow
   a. an opening in the wall, usually glass
   b. a spider
   c. a woman whose husband is dead

2. carton
   a. a funny picture
   b. a box made of heavy paper
   c. a cart on wheels

3. improve
   a. show something is right
   b. get or make better
   c. remember

4. owning
   a. having something that belongs to you
   b. needing to pay or repay money
   c. using the telephone

5. lonesome
   a. to lend something to someone
   b. feeling alone, or missing someone
   c. good-looking, attractive

6. blanket
   a. a bed cover
   b. an empty space
   c. a party

III. READING COMPREHENSION

Read the questions. Find the answers in the story. Write the answers under the questions.

1. How old is Mrs. Winter?

_____

_____

2. Why doesn't Mrs. Winter want a cat?

_____

_____

3. Dr. Kim is reading a medical magazine. What does it say?

_____

_____

4. When Mrs. Winter brings Sunshine home, what does the kitten do at first?

_____

_____

5. After Mrs. Winter puts both kittens in the bathroom, what do they do?

_____

_____

6. Why don't the kittens want to sleep in the bathroom?

_____

_____

IV. DISCUSSION

Look at the pictures. Talk to your partner. Use words from the story.

Picture #1
Where is Sunshine sleeping?
Where is Moonshine
sleeping?
We know that Mrs. Winter
doesn't sleep well.
Why is she sleeping now?

Picture #2
What is Dr. Kim doing?
At the beginning of the story, Dr. Kim is worried about
Mrs. Winter for various reasons. What are those reasons?
Why doesn't Mrs. Winter tell Dr. Kim about the kittens?

V. WRITING

In paragraph 3 of the story, there are two sentences which tell what Mrs. Winters remembers about Dr. Kim as a boy. Write those two sentences.

_____

_____

_____

_____

Every Saturday afternoon, thousands and thousands of people crowd into the arena.

The Lady or the Tiger
(from a story by Frank R. Stockton)

Dear Reader,

In another time, in a strange and wild country. . .

. . . there lives a King. Zegraf is his name. King Zegraf is handsome. He is as tall as a pine tree and as wide as a church door. His long hair is silver, like the moon in winter. His eyes are as dark as night.

Zegraf is rich and powerful. His soldiers often ride away to burn and kill for hundreds of miles around. They steal horses, gold and slaves. These they bring home to make King Zegraf even richer and more powerful.

The King seems to be more civilized, to have better manners, than many in his country. He wipes his mouth after he eats. He sometimes says 'please' and 'thank you'. But part of King Zagref is not civilized. Part of him is cruel. The people are afraid of him. When they meet him they bend their heads low. They look only as high as his knees because they are afraid of his cruel eyes.

King Zegraf knows how to read, a little. One of the slaves, whose name is Mathus, is teaching him. Together they read books about the great city of Rome. They read about the big, round theaters which the Romans call arenas. In these arenas, prisoners are forced to fight lions or other wild animals with their bare hands. The King likes this Roman idea. He thinks of a way to make it even better, even more cruel.

Slaves work day and night for seven years to build an arena for King Zegraf. When it is complete, it is just as big and just as beautiful as a Roman arena. But it is different...

Every Saturday afternoon, thousands and thousands of people crowd into the arena. The audience talks and laughs and eats fruit. Then the prisoner enters the arena in chains, and the audience becomes silent. The King leans back on his purple pillows and lifts one finger. That tells the soldiers to remove the prisoner's chains. The soldiers make the prisoner stand in front of two gold doors. The two doors look exactly the same, but everybody in the arena knows they are not. Behind one door sits a lovely lady. Behind the other waits a hungry tiger. Which door hides the tiger this Saturday? Which door hides the lady? People believe that only King Zegraf knows. If the prisoner is lucky and opens the correct door, he must immediately marry the lady. Even if he is already married. Even if he loves another woman. The audience is happy for the new husband and wife. If the prisoner opens the wrong door, the tiger jumps on him and begins to tear him apart. The audience enjoys that, too. Wrong door or right door, it's an exciting show. Nobody enjoys it more than the King.

The King has a daughter, Princess Zegranna. Like her father, she is tall and beautiful. Like her father, she has silver hair and dark eyes. Like her father, there is a little part of her that is cruel. But there is an important difference between the King and the Princess. The King is not able to love anybody. The Princess suddenly discovers that she can.

Mathus, the King's teacher, is almost as handsome as the King himself. But Mathus is kind and gentle, not cruel. He writes sad poems and he sings happy songs. Zegranna falls in love with Mathus and he with her. They want to marry.

When King Zegraf learns of this, he is as angry as thunder. How dare a slave dream of marrying his daughter? In the middle of the night, soldiers take Mathus to prison. Next Saturday, it is Mathus who is going to stand in front of the two gold doors. Next Saturday, it is Mathus who is going to have to choose — this door, or that one?

Princess Zegranna is not as powerful as her father, but she has some power. She also has gold and fine jewels. By Thursday, she is able to buy the information she needs. She now knows which door hides the lady this week, and which the tiger. All Thursday night, all Friday night, she walks up and down her rooms. She cannot eat, she cannot sleep. If she helps Mathus, if she saves his life, he must immediately marry the lady behind the door. That is the law. He has to live with her. Suppose he falls in love with her... Suppose they have a pretty baby who looks just like Mathus...

Zegranna thinks, "If I can't have Mathus, no other woman is going to have him." (Do you remember, Dear Reader, that Zegranna is a little bit cruel?)

Then she thinks, "My heart is going to break if I have to watch the tiger eat the man I love."

All night long she walks. She cannot decide what to do.

On Saturday, Zegranna sits next to her father in the arena. The crowd is especially noisy and excited. They know that the prisoner in chains is the man their Princess loves.

The soldiers bring in Mathus. He looks at Zegranna long and hard. He understands that only she can help him. He trusts her. Nobody except Mathus notices that Zegranna's finger moves a very little bit. It points to the left. Feeling confident, Mathus walks toward the gold doors. He opens the door on the left...

Dear Reader, which do you think comes out of that door — the lady or the tiger?

EXERCISES

I. VOCABULARY

You probably know many of these words from reading the story and looking at the pictures. If there are still some you don't know, look them up in your dictionary now.

powerful	married	crowd	civilized
confident	chains	notice	cruel
theater	audience	remove	arrested
steal	immediately	arena	

II. DEFINITIONS

Try to guess the best definition for these words. Then look them up in your dictionary and draw a circle around the answer.

1. steal
   a. a metal
   b. take something that does not belong to you
   c. an ocean animal

2. immediately
   a. right now
   b. later
   c. tomorrow

3. audience
   a. those who are in a play
   b. those who watch a play
   c. those who play games

4. remove
   a. move to a new house
   b. move back
   c. take away, or off

5. crowd
   a. a black bird
   b. a few people
   c. many people

6. civilized
   a. acts politely and has good manners
   b. has bad manners
   c. lives in Rome

III. READING COMPREHENSION

Read the questions. Find the answers in the story. Write the answers under the questions.

1. What happens in a Roman arena?

_____

_____

2. How is Mathus helping King Zegraf?

_____

_____

3. What happens every Saturday afternoon?

_____

_____

4. How is Mathus different from the King?

_____

_____

5. What is the important difference between Princess Zegranna and the King?

_____

_____

6. What is going to happen if Princess Zegranna saves Mathus from the tiger?

_____

_____

IV. DISCUSSION

Look at the pictures. Talk to your partner. Use words from the story.

Picture #1
Why is Princess Zegranna crying?
Why can't she decide what to do?

Picture #2
Why does Mathus decide to open the left door instead of the right door?
Why does Mathus believe that Zegranna is helping him?
Can we be sure that she is helping him? Give reasons for your answer.

V. WRITING

Write three things that King Zegraf's soldiers bring back when they ride away to kill and burn.

1. _____

2. _____

3. _____

Give two reasons why the King seems to be quite civilized.

1. _____

2. _____

Explain why the crowd is especially excited when the soldiers bring Mathus into the arena.

_____

_____

Ray loads their 1926 Chevrolet with pots and dishes, blankets and clothes.
He ties two mattresses to the roof of the car.

A Valentine for Mama

In 1935, Ray Freeman's farm blows away. Ray's farm is in Oklahoma. For five years, beginning in 1931, it hardly rains there at all. The earth dries up and becomes dust. Then the wind-storms come, day after day, and blow the dust away. Those parts of Oklahoma and Kansas where this happens are called the Dust Bowl. Between 1934 and 1940, over a million people leave the Dust Bowl. In their broken-down cars and trucks they drive west on Route 66 to California. There they hope to get jobs picking fruit or cotton. They are sure everything is going to be better in California.

Ray Freeman tries to keep his farm as long as he can. But he can't grow wheat anymore and the dust buries his pigs and chickens. One day he gets a letter from his bank about the money he owes them and can't pay. In thirty days they're going to take his land. Ray and his wife Amy talk until late at night, trying to decide the best thing to do.

"Lots of Okies are going to California," Ray reminds Amy. 'Okie' is the name Oklahoma people call themselves. "I want us to go too," Ray says. "I want a job. I want my family to have the things that other people have. Look at our daughter Mary. She's nine years old and pretty as a picture, but she only has one dress, and it's too small. What hurts me is that she never complains, never asks for anything, never expects anything. And Jimmy, he's only four, but he's learning not to expect anything, either."

Amy agrees they need to go to California. But she has a problem. "My Pa is sick and close to dying. I can't leave him to die alone in a rented room. You and the kids start without me. The kids can stay with my sister in Arizona while you're looking for a job in California. It's not going to be very long before you and I and the kids are together again."

The Freemans sell all the furniture they can before the bank sends a man to take their farm. Then Ray packs their 1926 Chevrolet with pots and dishes, blankets and clothes. He ties two mattresses to the roof of the car. Saying goodbye to Mama is hard for everyone. Mary holds on to her mother tightly until Ray gently pulls her away.

Ray and the children are on their way to Texas. Ray plans to work as they travel to earn money for food and gas. Sometimes he gets work, cutting wood or painting a barn, but not often. It is the time of the Great Depression, as it is called. Everywhere people are looking for jobs that don't exist. Ray is worried. The trip is taking too long. The kids look tired, thin and dirty. In New Mexico, during Christmas, the car breaks down. Another Okie kindly helps Ray fix it, but ten days pass before they are on the road again. The nights are very cold. Ray wraps himself and the children in all their blankets and they try to sleep together in the back of the car.

Jimmy always says, "Pa, tell again how it's going to be in California."

Ray tells how good life is going to be, but he's not sure he believes it any more. He hears that Okies are not welcome in California.

One day they drive up to a country store for gas. Ray gives Mary a quarter to buy bread and milk. In the store, Mary sees pretty valentine cards with red hearts. One of them says, "To Mother" and shows a young woman with her two children in a flower garden. The card costs ten cents. Mary knows what she is doing is wrong, she knows Pa is going to be angry, but she misses her mother so much. She returns to the car with bread and the valentine.

Ray is very angry. "We don't even have a spare tire for the car and you buy a valentine? Take it back and get milk. Do as I say and do it now!" Mary obeys her father. She doesn't cry, but she doesn't say anything the rest of the day. Ray is silent too.

Even Jimmy is quiet. He looks very small and lonely. That night, when they are all under the blankets together, Jimmy says, "Pa, tell about California," but Ray doesn't feel like talking.

After the kids fall asleep, Ray looks out at the dark sky, thinking. Is life really going to be better for his family in California? Who can say? Right now they are poor and homeless. Ray regrets getting angry at Mary. He knows she misses Amy as much as he does. Maybe, Ray thinks, there are times when a valentine is more important than bread or milk or even a spare tire.

The next morning they cross into Arizona. Ray stops in the first town. It's just a little town, but there is a store.

"Mary," Ray says, "here's a dime. Go buy a valentine for Mama."

Mary doesn't find the same card, but she buys one that is almost as nice. Ray and Mary sign it and so does Jimmy, with a little help. They put a three-cent stamp on the envelope and mail it to Mama, way back in Oklahoma.

That night, when they are under the blankets and Jimmy asks for a story about California, Ray agrees. He always begins the story the same way.

"We're going to have a little house, a white house with a white fence. There's going to be an orange tree in our yard, and a lemon tree, too. Any time you want lemonade, you just go out and pick some lemons. And I'm going to have a job, and a pay check every Friday. We're going to send your Mama a ticket to come to California on the train. We're all going to go to the station to meet her wearing our fine new clothes from a department store..."

Ray sees that the children are asleep. He thinks about Amy. He imagines her opening her valentine and smiling. For the first time in a long while, he smiles too.

EXERCISES

I. VOCABULARY

You probably know many of these words from reading the story and looking at the pictures. If there are still some you don't know, look them up in your dictionary now.

wheat	complain	bury (buries)	barn
mattress	furniture	silent	believe
obey	regret	imagine	bowl
dust	either	heart	

II. DEFINITIONS

Try to guess the best definition for these words. Then look them up in your dictionary and draw a circle around the answer.

1. bury (buries)
   a. fruit
   b. cover with earth
   c. plant

2. regret
   a. go back
   b. a large bird
   c. feel sorry

3. dust
   a. earth that is dry and fine
   b. a brush
   c. wash the floor

4. obey
   a. a musical instrument
   b. accept a command or order
   c. a body of water

5. wheat
   a. the opposite of black
   b. high temperature
   c. grain used to make bread.

6. silent
   a. making no sound
   b. noisy
   c. made out of silk

III. READING COMPREHENSION

Read the questions. Find the answers in the story. Write the answers under the questions.

1. Ray Freeman gets a letter from his bank. What is the letter about?

_____

_____

2. What do the people who leave the Dust Bowl hope to get in California?

_____

_____

3. Why doesn't Amy go to California with her family?

_____

_____

4. What does the word 'Okie' mean?

_____

_____

5. What does Ray plan to do while he and the children are driving to Texas?

_____

_____

6. What does Ray hope to send to Amy after he finds a job in California?

_____

_____

IV. DISCUSSION

Look at the pictures. Talk to
your partner. Use words from
the story.

Picture #1
What is Mary thinking about
when she looks at the valentine
cards?
Why does she know it is wrong
to buy the valentine?
Why does she buy it anyway?

Picture #2
Where are Ray and the children?
What are they doing?
Is this really happening?
Do you think it is going to happen?

V. WRITING

Beginning in 1931, certain things happen that turn parts of Oklahoma and Kansas into a Dust Bowl. List three of them.

1. _____

2. _____

3. _____

Rigoberta Menchu accepts the Nobel Peace Prize dressed in clothes
that are typical of her people.

Rigoberta Menchu, a Woman of Peace

The Nobel Peace Prize is the highest prize the world has to offer. President Woodrow Wilson, Mother Teresa, and Dr. Martin Luther King Jr. are among the winners.

The Peace Prize is not given every year. When it is given, it is always on December 10, at the University of Oslo in Norway. The royal families of Norway and Sweden and important people from every country attend the ceremony. Reporters and television cameras crowd close to the stage.

In 1992, thirty-three year old Rigoberta Menchu, from Guatemala, wins the Nobel Peace Prize. She is a Quiche Maya Indian, and she wins it for her brave work in defending the rights of Indian peoples. She accepts the prize — a gold medal and more than a million dollars — dressed in clothes that are typical of her people. When it is time for her to speak, she is quiet for a moment, remembering...

She is five years old. She and her mother and the older children are riding in a truck with a few other Indian families. Their father, a farmer, remains at home in the mountains to work on their poor, rocky land. But the mother and children must earn money on a far-away *finca*, or plantation, where sugar, coffee or cotton is grown. By the time she is eight, Rigoberta can pick thirty-five pounds of coffee beans a day. That year, her baby brother dies of hunger. Another brother dies when chemicals are dropped on the cotton field from an airplane while people are still working there. Of Rigoberta's ten brothers and sisters, only four are still living today.

Rigoberta does not go to school. She does not learn to read until she is almost grown. Most Indians speak their own languages but do not speak Spanish. They do not understand that the government is supposed to represent them, too. They think the government is only for rich people.

Rigoberta grows up hungry and afraid. She is afraid that these rich people are going to steal her home. They always come, with soldiers, to take away

Indian lands. The government helps them do it. While she is still a young girl, Rigoberta joins other poor Indians to work together in the long, hard battle for justice.

Like her father, Vincente, Rigoberta is a very religious Christian. She follows the teaching of Jesus every day of her life. She also follows Indian tradition that respects all living things.

Vincente Menchu cannot read or write. He speaks only a little Spanish. Yet he becomes an underground leader in the C.U.C., the United Committee of *Campesinos*, or poor farmers. With the help of workers and students they fight for a better life in Guatemala.

Vincente is always in danger. He spends long years in prison. Yet his daughter Rigoberta is not afraid to join her father in his work with the Campesinos. In 1979, she becomes a member of the C.U.C. She leaves her beloved mountains to go wherever she is needed. She learns to speak Spanish. She learns the languages of different Indian groups. Rigoberta is a good organizer. She teaches Indians how to defend their villages, sometimes only with sticks and stones and knives.

Rigoberta's sixteen-year old brother also works for the C.U.C. The police arrest him and beat him almost to death. They finally kill him by pouring gasoline over him and setting him on fire. Rigoberta's heart breaks for her brother, but she continues to work and organize.

In January 1980, Vincente Menchu is one of many who march to Guatemala City. They want to call attention to their cause, so some of them break into the offices of the Spanish Ambassador. Guatemalan police attack the building. Whether it is an accident or not, no one knows. A fire starts, and Vincente and his friends die. So do the officials of the Spanish government who are in the building. Now the world pays attention to the struggle in Guatemala and to the hundred thousand who are already dead because of that struggle.

The police begin to hunt for the rest of Vincente Menchu's family. They catch Rigoberta's mother and she dies a terrible death. Rigoberta is able to escape to Mexico. She returns to Guatemala secretly, several times, but always with bodyguards. From Mexico she continues the work which later brings her the Nobel Peace Prize.

Rigoberta Menchu now uses her prize money to defend the rights of native peoples. She does this in memory of her father and in his name.

EXERCISES

I. VOCABULARY

You probably know many of these words from reading the story and looking at the pictures. If there are still some you don't know, look them up in your dictionary now.

defend	escape	earn	bodyguards
committee	quiet	organizer	prize
camera	hunger (hungry)	attend	brave
cotton	underground (under + ground)		

II. DEFINITIONS:

Try to guess the best definitions for these words. Then look them up in your dictionary and draw a circle around the answer.

1. cotton
    a. a small bed
    b. a plant used to make thread
    c. two thousand pounds

2. accept
    a. take or receive
    b. exclude
    c. a tool

3. hunger
    a. something to put clothes on
    b. a shed or shelter for airplanes
    c. pain caused by need of food

4. earn
    a. a vase
    b. a bird
    c. make money by working

5. escape
    a. a coat without sleeves
    b. to get away
    c. to bake in a sauce

6. quiet
    a. to stop
    b. completely
    c. making no sound

III. READING COMPREHENSION

Read the questions. Find the answers in the story. Write the answers under the questions.

1. When and where is the Nobel Peace Prize given?

_____

_____

2. What can Rigoberta Menchu do by the time she is eight years old?

_____

_____

3. Why does Rigoberta begin to hate rich people?

_____

_____

4. In what way is Rigoberta like her father, Vincente?

_____

_____

5. What is Rigoberta able to do after the police catch her mother?

_____

_____

6. Why does Rigoberta Menchu win the Nobel Peace Prize?

_____

_____

IV. DISCUSSION

Look at the pictures. Talk to your partners. Use words from the story.

Picture #1
Where are the Indian families in the truck going?
Do you think Rigoberta's father is in the truck? Why not?
Do you think the Indian children in the truck are going to go to school?
Do most of the Indians in the truck speak Spanish?

Picture #2
What is wrong with what is happening in this picture?
Rigoberta's brother is in this cotton field. What happens to him?
How many of Rigoberta's ten brothers and sisters are living today?

V. WRITING

The story says that Rigoberta is a good organizer. List four things she does that make her a good organizer.

1. _____

2. _____

3. _____

4. _____

He looks on his desk for his glasses. They are not there. They are not in the desk drawers. They are not in his shirt pocket. Where can they be?

The Absent-Minded Professor

Dr. Otto Franz is a professor of philosophy. He is a good teacher and a kind man. His students love him, but they sometimes laugh at him. They call him the absent-minded professor because he is always forgetting something. All his students have funny stories to tell about him.

Dr. Franz's mind is in the clouds. He is so busy thinking important thoughts that he doesn't remember to get a haircut. He pays no attention to clothes and often comes to class wearing two socks of different colors. One evening, students see him walking around and around the parking lot. As he walks, he talks to himself. He can't remember where his car is parked. He's not even sure it's in the parking lot. Does he bring his car on Thursdays, he wonders? Or is it Wednesdays he doesn't drive? What day is today, anyway?

This morning, Profesor Franz has no classes to teach. He plans to stay in his office and read examination papers. He works hard for a few hours. Then his eyes get tired. He pushes his glasses up on top of his head, as it is his habit to do. Then he leans back in his chair and rubs his eyes. "A cup of coffee," Dr. Franz thinks, "is exactly what I need right now."

In the university coffee shop, Dr. Franz meets another professor and they talk for a while. Then a student asks him for advice, which he gladly gives. Three cups of coffee later, he returns to his office, ready to work again.

He looks on his desk for his glasses. They are not there. They are not in the desk drawers. They are not in his shirt pocket. Where can they be? "Maybe they are at home," Dr. Franz thinks. Then he decides that is not possible. "Don't you remember," he asks himself, "looking high and low for your glasses, right here in this office, this very morning? Don't you remember going back to the car to look for them? Don't you remember finally finding them in your lunch box, under your turkey sandwich, next to your orange? That answers that question. My glasses are not at home. So where are they?"

"Now, let's be reasonable about this," Dr. Franz tells himself. "Glasses don't disappear into the air. They are real. They are objects. A real object can't be **nowhere**, it has to be **somewhere.** It's only a matter of using my mind to discover where. I just have to think calmly." He thinks. "Is it possible," he wonders, "for someone to come into this office to steal something? Certainly it's possible. But why my glasses? Why not steal my money, which is right here in my jacket pocket? And my jacket is hanging on my chair where anyone can see it." Then Dr. Franz remembers that his money is not in his jacket pocket but in his pants pocket.

"Okay," he argues with himself, "a thief comes in here looking for money, but there isn't any. So he takes my glasses. No, Otto, it doesn't make sense. What good are your glasses to him? Unless...yes, unless he is a poor person who needs glasses but doesn't have the money to buy them. Wait a minute. What reason is there to believe that my glasses, with my prescription, fit his eyes? Not a single reason in the world. Correct? No, Otto Franz! Not correct. There is a reason, the best possible reason. He takes the glasses, doesn't he? That proves that the glasses fit him, otherwise why take them? That's it. That's the explanation."

Satisfied, the professor turns back to his work. He makes notes on the examination papers with his right hand. His left hand pushes his glasses from the top of his head, where they are sitting all this time, back down to his nose. He doesn't even notice. Once, while he works, his thoughts return to the man (he's sure it's a man) who now has his glasses. If the fellow wears glasses, where are his own glasses? Lost, Professor Franz decides. Either lost or stolen.

"Poor man," the professor thinks, "I hope my glasses make his life a little easier."

That night, Dr. Franz is at home, watching the news on television. Then he wants to see a different program. Absent-minded, as usual, he reaches for his pocket calculator and starts pushing buttons. Nothing happens. He is still watching the news. He looks closely at the instrument in his hand. It is black. It has black buttons with white numbers. So why doesn't it change the program? "Because it's not the TV control," he explains to himself. "It's a pocket calculator. Otto, I sometimes think that you are getting a little absent-minded."

While he is watching TV, he notices that he has a spot on one of the lenses of his glasses. He takes his glasses off, blows on them, and rubs them with his handkerchief. Suddenly he realizes what he is holding in his hands. "My goodness," the professor says in happy surprise, "I have my glasses back! I guess that poor man doesn't need them after all."

EXERCISES

I. VOCABULARY

You probably know many of these words from reading the story and looking at the pictures. If there are still some you don't know, look them up in your dictionary now.

attention	habit	nowhere	philosophy
thief	reasonable	object	push
absent	final(ly)	drawer	calculator
fellow	satisfied	lens	

II. DEFINITIONS

Try to guess the best definitions for these words. Then look them up in your dictionary and draw a circle around the answer.

1. lens
   a. lets someone borrow something
   b. bends backward or forward
   c. a piece of glass used to correct vision

2. habit
   a. a small animal
   b. a place where plants or animals naturally live
   c. to act often in a certain way

3. nowhere
   a. not any place
   b. here now
   c. doesn't listen

4. calculator
   a. carries people from one level to another
   b. a machine for doing mathematical operations
   c. a moving stairway

5. fellow
   a. to go or come after
   b. supports the head during sleep
   c. a man

6. absent
   a. away, not here
   b. something sent by mail
   c. funny, unreasonable

III. READING COMPREHENSION

Read the questions. Find the answers in the story. Write the answers under the question.

1. What happens because the professor pays no attention to clothes?

_____

_____

2. What does Professor Franz do in the university coffee shop?

_____

_____

3. Dr. Franz has a habit of doing something. What is that habit?

_____

_____

4. What does Professor Franz say about real objects?

_____

_____

5. Is Dr. Franz's money in his jacket pocket? Where is it?

_____

_____

6. What does the professor say that shows he is not angry with the thief he believes has his glasses?

_____

_____

IV. DISCUSSION

Look at the pictures. Talk to your partner. Use words from the story.

Picture #1
Why is Dr. Franz sure his glasses
are not at home?
Where does he finally find his
glasses when he thinks, earlier in
the morning, that they are lost?

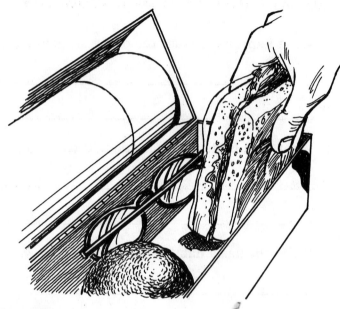

Picture #2
What is the professor holding in his hand?
What does this instrument do?
What does he think it is?
Why does he think so?

V. WRITING

There are three sentences in the story that describe how Dr. Franz discovers he has his glasses again. Write those three sentences.

1. _____

_____

2. _____

_____

3. _____

_____

Sasha cuts the last string of the package and there stands the work of art.

A Work of Art
(Adapted from a story by Anton Chekhov)

Dr. Andrei Rostov is surprised to see Sasha Smirnov in his waiting room. Sasha is a handsome boy, fourteen years old. He is carrying a big package.

"Sasha," the kind old doctor says, "I hope you are not sick again."

Sasha replies, "I am now completely well, dear Doctor, but only because of you. My mother and I can never thank you enough for saving my life. We are ashamed that we do not have the money to pay you. Instead, we beg you to accept this present, which is a truly great work of art."

Sasha begins to unwrap the package.

"No, no, no — please!" Dr. Rostov says. "That isn't necessary. I am used to patients who can't pay. I don't want you to give me a great work of art."

Sasha doesn't listen. He continues to remove the wrapping paper and string. "Of course, you know," he says as he works, "that my mother buys and sells old furniture and art. That is her business. And my mother thinks that this is an especially fine piece. There is only one other exactly like it in the world. In fact, they are intended to be a pair. It is so sad that nobody knows where the second one is."

"Sasha," Dr. Rostov interrupts, "I can't accept a present of such value."

But Sasha cuts the last string of the package and there stands the work of art: two women who are not wearing any clothes and are holding a lamp over their heads.

For a little while, the doctor is speechless. He finally says, "Sasha, you must understand that I cannot have this...this whatever it is...in here. Many of my patients are women and they are going to think...I don't know what they are going to think."

"Surely, Dr. Rostov," Sasha says, "great art is more important than what some women think. Besides, if you don't accept our present, my mother and I are going to be deeply, deeply hurt."

The doctor does not want to hurt Sasha and his mother, so he has to accept. He thanks Sasha as politely as he can. After the boy leaves, he wonders what he is going to do about this unwelcome possession. Maybe he can give it to someone else. In his mind, he makes a list of all his friends. For one or another reason, none of them is right until he remembers Igor. His friend Igor Ukhov, a school teacher, is not married and lives alone. Dr. Rostov decides that the work of art is a perfect present for an unmarried man. He hurries over to Igor's apartment.

Igor does not seem to be very pleased with the present. He says he doesn't want it. "My mother visits me often." he says. "I can't keep it here!"

"Hide it when your mother comes," Dr. Rostov advises. He leaves the apartment quickly, before Igor can try to give the present back to him.

Igor Ukhov looks at the two women with the lamp. He thinks, "I don't care if it's a work of art or not a work of art. I have to get it out of here before Mama sees it."

What can he do with it? Whom can he give it to? Immediately he thinks of his friend, Nikita Denisov, whose birthday is tomorrow. Nikita is an actor. He and his actor friends are always having wild parties and doing wild things. Nikita is really going to love this birthday present, Igor tells himself. Still, just to be safe, Igor takes it to Nikita's house when he is certain his friend is not at home. He leaves it with a note explaining that it is an important work of art. He also wishes Nikita a happy birthday.

Nikita comes home late with a few other actors and actresses from the theater. He finds the present and reads the note.

"Igor thinks this is an important work of art," he says. "As usual, he's wrong. It's terrible. I hate it. The women holding up the lamp are too fat. Now, beautiful women — that's a different matter. In honor of my birthday, I'm going to throw this ugly thing away."

"Don't do that," one of his friends tells him. "There's a woman in town, Anna Smirnova, who buys and sells old furniture and art. Maybe you can get a little money for your 'ugly thing'. Money is always useful."

A few days later, Sasha returns to Dr. Rostov's office carrying a large package.

"I have the most wonderful surprise!" he says. "I'm sure you remember that the work of art, which is now yours, is one of a pair. Well, I still cannot believe our good luck! This morning, a man walks into my mother's store offering to sell the other, the **second** one of the pair! Of course my mother buys it right away — for you! We want you to have them both. It makes us so happy to know that you now own the complete set."

Dr. Rostov opens his mouth to say something, but no sound comes out. His power to speak seems to be gone.

EXERCISES

I. VOCABULARY

You probably know many of these words from reading the story and looking at the pictures. If there are still some you don't know, look them up in your dictionary now.

ashamed	present	wrap(ping)	intend(ed)
speech	string	possession	hide
honor	useful	pair	set
package	used (to)	accept	

II. DEFINITIONS

Try to guess the best definition for these words. Then look them up in your dictionary and draw a circle around the answer.

1. pair
   a. a fruit
   b. two that are the same
   c. three that are the same

2. possession
   a. something that is owned
   b. a march or parade
   c. a place or location

3. used (to)
   a. a purpose
   b. finished
   c. accustomed (to)

4. wrap
   a. make a noise
   b. tear
   c. cover with paper

5. honor
   a. a judge
   b. show respect
   c. make sharp

6. hide
   a. throw something away
   b. put something up high
   c. put something where it can't be seen

III. READING COMPREHENSION

Read the questions. Find the answers in the story. Write the answers under the questions.

1. What kind of business does Sasha's mother have?

_____

_____

2. Sasha tells Dr. Rostov that the work of art is one of a pair. Where is the second one?

_____

_____

3. Why does Dr. Rostov finally accept the present?

_____

_____

4. Why does Dr. Rostov decide to give the present to Igor Ukhov?

_____

_____

5. Why does Igor decide to give the present to Nikita?

_____

_____

6. Nikita says he hates the work of art. What reason does he give?

_____

_____

IV. DISCUSSION

Look at the pictures. Talk to your partner. Use words from the story.

Picture #1
Tell what you know about Nikita and his friends.
What does Nikita want to do with the present?
What does his friend advise him to do?
Who is Anna Smirnova?

Picture #2
What is Sasha's wonderful surprise?
There is something about the present Sasha is now giving Dr. Rostov that Sasha does not know. What are the facts he does not know?
How does Dr. Rostov feel about Sasha's wonderful surprise?

V. WRITING

Dictation. Study the third paragraph on Page One beginning with the words, **"Sasha replies . . . "** Think about spelling and about punctuation. Close your book as the teacher dictates. Then open your book and check your work.

_____

_____

_____

_____

_____

This comprehensive word list includes vocabulary from the stories which might be new to some advanced primary level students. Cognates of Spanish are here marked "C." Words found in the *Oxford Picture Dictionary of American English* are marked "O." Those found in Robert J. Dixson's *The 2,000 Most Frequently Used Words In English* are marked "D."

A

Word	C	O	D
able			D
absent	C		D
accept	C		D
accident	C		D
advice	C		D
afraid			D
agree			D
alike			D
angry			D
animal	C	O	D
anxious	C		D
apology	C		D
arena	C		D
argue			D
arrest	C		D
arrive			D
arrow			D
ashamed			D
astronomy	C		
attend			D
attention	C		D
authority	C		D

B

Word	C	O	D
backward			D
bag		O	D
basket			D
behind		O	D
belief			D
believe			D
belong			D
bench		O	
blanket		O	D
bodyguard			D
book		O	
bottom			D
bowl		O	D
box		O	D
bracelet	C	O	
brave			D
bread		O	D
breakfast			D
breath			D
breathe			D
bring			D
bullet		O	D
bury			D
busy			D

C

Word	C	O	D
cake		O	D
calculator	C	O	D
calf		O	
candy		O	D
card(s)	C	O	D
carpenter	C	O	
carton	C	O	D
cat		O	D
cent	C		D
century			D
certain	C		D
cheaper			D
cheek		O	D
chicken		O	D
choose			D
civilized	C		D
clean		O	D
close		O	
closet		O	D
cloth		O	D
comfortable	C		D
command	C		D
committee	C		D

Word	C	O	D
complain			D
complicated	C		D
confidence	C		
confuse			D
consider	C		D
constitution	C		
control			D
cook		O	D
cotton		O	D
country		O	D
crowd			D
cruel	C		D
cry			D
curious	C		D
customer		O	D
cut		O	D

D

Word	C	O	D
daughter		O	D
daughter-in-law			D
decide	C		D
delicious	C		D
disagree			D
disappear	C		D
disappointed			D
distance	C		D
doctor	C	O	D
drawer		O	D
dry		O	D
dust		O	D

E

Word	C	O	D
eager			D
earn			D
earth		O	D
easy			D
economical	C		

	C	O	D
either			D
elevator			D
embroider		O	
empty		O	D
enjoy			D
enough			D
enter	C		D
entire	C		D
escape	C		D
especially	C		D
event			D
excited	C		D
excuse	C		D
expect			D
expensive			D
experience	C		D
explain	C		D
expression	C		D

F

	C	O	D
familiar	C		
family	C	O	D
famous	C		D
far			D
farm		O	D
fellow			D
finally	C		D
find			D
finish			D
fire		O	D
flood			D
floor		O	D
fool			D
forest		O	D
forget			D
free			D
freeway		O	D
friend			D
friendly			D
frighten			D
front		O	D
furniture		O	D

G

	C	O	D
giant	C		D
glad			D
glasses		O	
gold			D
gone			D
government	C		D
group	C		D
grow			D
guard	C		D
guess			D

H

	C	O	D
habit	C		D
hammer		O	
hand		O	D
handsome			D
happy			D
hate			D
head		O	D
health			D
heart		O	D
heel		O	D
hero	C		D
hit		O	D
honor	C		D
hopeless			D
horse		O	D
hour		O	D
hungry			D
husband		O	D

I

	C	O	D
idea	C		D
imagine	C		D
immediately	C		D
impatient	C		D
important	C		D
improve			D
insurance			D
intelligent	C		
intend	C		D
interrupt	C		D
invisible	C		

J

	C	O	D
jacket	C	O	
job			D
joke			D
just	C		

K

	C	O	D
key			D
kick			D
kind			D
kitten		O	D
knock			D

L

	C	O	D
land			D
laugh		O	D
leg		O	D
lens			O
license	C	O	
lie			D
light			D
lone			D
lonely			D
lonesome			D
loom			D
loosen			D
lost			D
loud			D
lucky			D

M

	C	O	D
machine	C		D
matter			D
mattress		O	D
measure		O	D
menu	C	O	D
merchant	C		D
middle		O	D
minister	C		
mistake			D
month		O	D
moon		O	D
mother		O	D
move	C		D
mysterious	C		D

N

	C	O	D
neighbor		O	D
nervous	C		D
notice	C		D
nowhere			D
number		O	D

O

	C	O	D
obey	C		D
object	C		D
occupied	C		
office	C	O	D
officer	C	O	D
old		O	D
only			D
operator	C	O	D
opinion	C		D
opportunity	C		D
orange			D
order	C		D
ordinary	C		D
organizer	C		
oven		O	D
own			D

P

	C	O	D
package	C	O	D
pair	C		D
paper	C	O	D
passenger	C	O	D
path		O	
patient	C	O	D
pattern	C	O	D
payment			D
pepper		O	D
philosophy	C		D
physics	C		
piece	C	O	D
plain			D
plan	C		D
plate	C	O	D
pleasure	C		D
poor			D
popular	C		D
possession	C		D
present	C		D
pressure	C		D
pretend	C		
private	C		D
prize			D
problem	C		D
promise	C		D
prove	C		D
pull			D

Q

	C	O	D
quarrel			D
queen		O	D
question			D
quick			D
quiet	C		D

R

	C	O	D
racing			D
rain		O	D
rare	C		D
rate			D
reach			D
reasonable	C		D
recognize	C		D
regret			D
religious	C		D
remember			D
remind			D
repair	C	O	
repeat	C		D
require	C		D
rescue			D
restaurant	C	O	D
revolve	C		D
reward			D
rich	C		D
rights			D
ring		O	D
roof		O	D
rule			D

S

	C	O	D
sad(ly)			D
salesman		O	D
save			D
science	C	O	D
scratch			D
send			D
serious	C		D
set			D
shine			D
shirt		O	D
shop		O	D
short cut			D
shout(s)		O	D
sick			D
sign			D
signal	C		D
silent	C		D
skirt		O	D
smell			D
smile			D
smooth			D
soft drink		O	
somehow			D
son		O	D
sorry			D
soup	C		D
spare			D
speak			D
speech			D
spill			D
star		O	D
steal			D
step		O	D
stomach	C	O	D
string			D
stupid	C		D
suddenly			D
summer			D
sun		O	D
supermarket	C	O	
supposed			D
surprise	C		D
surround			D
sweet			D
sympathy	C		D
system	C		D

T

	C	O	D
taste			D
temperature	C		D
theater	C	O	D
thermometer	C	O	
thief			D
think			D
thread			D
ticket		O	D
toe		O	D
towel	C	O	D
travel		O	D
trick			D
trouble			D
truck		O	
truckdriver		O	
true			D

U

	C	O	D
ugly			D
understand			D
unhappy			D
uniform	C	O	
used to			D
useful			D
usual	C		

V

	C	O	D
vegetable	C	O	D
village			D
visit	C		D
voice	C		D

W

	C	O	D
wait			D
waste			D
weak			D
wear			D
weather		O	D
weave		O	
weight		O	D
wheat		O	D
whisper			D
whole			D
widow			D
winter		O	D
wonderful			D
worry (ies)			D
wrap			D
wrong			D

XYZ

	C	O	D
year			D
yellow			D
yet			D
young			D

EXERCISE ANSWER KEY

Chapter 1.
A BIG BOWL OF MENUDO
Exercise II

1. a   4. b
2. b   5. c
3. c   6. a

Exercise III

1. Fay has no experience as a waitress.
2. The only thing he ever orders is a big bowl of menudo.
3. He's a nice man and a good dentist, but he can be difficult.
4. She waits for him to begin eating, but he does not.
   or/ He just sits, looking at his bowl.
5. He wants her to taste it.
6. There is no spoon.

Chapter 2.
THE FLAT TIRE
Exercise II

1. b   4. b
2. b   5. c
3. a   6. a

Exercise III

1. He has an appointment with the farmer who may buy insurance.
2. The car begins to make a funny noise. It goes bump, bump, bumping along.
3. You loosen and unscrew the lug nuts that connect the wheel to the car.
4. He says, "I don't like people watching me make a fool of myself."
5. A tiny old woman in a pink raincoat and a yellow rainhat.
6. The last thing he wants is advice from a patient in a mental hospital.

Chapter 3.
SWEETIE'S WASHING MACHINE
Exercise II

1. b   4. a
2. c   5. b
3. a   6. c

Exercise III

1. She needs one hundred and sixteen dollars. Her washing machine is broken. That's how much it costs to fix it.
2. She wants to read to Tanya and play with her in the park.
3. She has an invitation to a party. She wants to buy a new dress.
4. Sweetie's smile is brave and bright.
5. She is going to get paper money. She doesn't want to pay the washing machine repair man with nickels, dimes and quarters.
6. Harry doesn't swing his tail when Tanya pets him.
   or /Harry doesn't even open his eyes.

Chapter 4.
THERE IS ROOM FOR ONE MORE
Exercise II

1. c   4. c
2. b   5. a
3. b   6. c

Exercise III

1. She can see that there are four or five passengers.
2. There is nothing but moonlight on the driveway.
3. She begins to feel better.
4. They are just ordinary people like herself.
5. She keeps remembering the strange things that are happening to her.

6. Outside, hundreds of people are standing around.
   or/ Ambulances and police cars are arriving.

Chapter 5.
MRS. WRIGHT AND MR. WRONG
Exercise II
1. b
2. a
3. c
4. c
5. c
6. a

Exercise III
1. Sally is Albert's sister.
2. The clouds blow away and the sun comes out.
3. She takes a long time to get dressed.
4. Albert drives faster than usual because they are so late.
5. He asks to see Albert's driver's license.
6. He has enough trouble already.

Chapter 6.
THE TRIAL OF GALILEO
Exercise II
1. a
2. b
3. b
4. c
5. b
6. a

Exercise III
1. He is on trial because of what he thinks.
   or/ He disagreees with a belief of the Catholic Church.
2. He proves that they all fall at the same speed.
3. Copernicus believes that the sun, not the earth, is the center of a great, complicated astronomical system.
   or/ Copernicus believes that the moon and the planets, which include the earth, revolve around the sun.
4. He suggests that our universe may be only one of many.

5. He is warned not to believe or teach the ideas of Copernicus.
6. The Catholic Church tells the world that the mistakes of the Church against Galileo must be honestly admitted.

Chapter 7.
THE EMPEROR'S NEW CLOTHES
Exercise II
1. b
2. c
3. a
4. c
5. a
6. b

Exercise III
1. He is cutting the Emperor's hair in the latest style.
2. He says, "I like him. I have a feeling he is going to make us rich."
3. He says, "Then I can finally know which of my ministers is wise and which is a fool."
4. Hans pretends to hold a long piece of cloth over his arm.
5. It looks like nothing, like air.
6. The little girl says, "Mommy, the Emperor isn't wearing any clothes!"
   or/ "He's out in the street in his underwear!"

Chapter 8.
YELLOW BIRD AND THE SEVEN BROTHERS
Exercise II
1. c
2. b
3. a
4. b
5. c
6. a

Exercise III
1. Each buffalo blanket she makes has bright, wonderful colors.
   or/ Each one is embroidered with unusual patterns of beads and feathers.

2. This one is smaller than the others.
   or/ It is a shirt for a young boy.
3. She comes to the tipi she sees every night in her dreams.
4. Their leader is the biggest buffalo in the world.
5. They cause the tree to grow a thousand feet in less than a minute.
6. They are able to step off into the clouds.

Chapter 9.
SUNSHINE, MOONSHINE AND MRS.WINTER
Exercise II
1. c   4. a
2. b   5. b
3. b   6. a

Exercise III
1. She is closer to seventy than she is to sixty.
2. Cats scratch the furniture.
3. It says that owning a cat often improves the health of older people.
4. For a while the kitten just sits there, examining everything with her perfectly round eyes.
5. They begin to cry and scratch at the door.
6. They think Mrs. Winter is their mother. They want to sleep with her.

Chapter 10
THE LADY OR THE TIGER
Exercise II
1. b   4. c
2. a   5. c
3. b   6. a

Exercise III
1. Prisoners are forced to fight lions or other wild animals with their bare hands.

2. Mathus is teaching King Zegraf how to read.
3. Every Saturday afternoon, thousands and thousands of people crowd into the arena.
4. Mathus is kind and gentle, not cruel.
5. The King is not able to love anybody. The Princess suddenly discovers that she can.
6. He must immediately marry the lady behind the door.

Chapter 11.
A VALENTINE FOR MAMA
Exercise II
1. b   4. b
2. c   5. c
3. a   6. a

Exercise III
1. The letter is about the money he owes them and can't pay.
2. They hope to get jobs picking fruit or cotton.
3. She has a problem.
   or/ She says, "My Pa is sick and close to dying. I can't leave him to die alone in a rented room."
4. 'Okie' is the name Oklahoma people call themselves.
5. Ray plans to work as they travel to earn money for gas and food.
6. He hopes to send her a ticket to come to California on the train.

Chapter 12
RIGOBERTA MENCHU, A WOMAN OF PEACE
Exercise II
1. b   4. c
2. a   5. b
3. c   6. c

Exercise III

1. The Nobel Peace Prize is given on December 10, at the University of Oslo in Norway.
2. She can pick thirty-five pounds of coffee beans a day.
3. She is afraid rich people are going to steal her home.
4. Like her father, Vincente, Rigoberta is a very religious Christian. or/ Rigoberta is not afraid to join her father in his work with the Campesinos.
5. She is able to escape to Mexico.
6. She wins it for her brave work in defending the rights of Indian peoples.

Chapter 13.
THE ABSENT-MINDED PROFESSOR

Exercise II

1.	c	4.	b
2.	c	5.	c
3.	a	6.	a

Exercise III

1. He often comes to class wearing two socks of different color.
2. He meets another professor and they talk for a while.
   or/ A student asks him for advice which he gladly gives.
3. He pushes his glasses up on top of his head.
4. He says, "A real object can't be **nowhere** it has to be **somewhere**."
5. His money is not in his jacket pocket but in his pants pocket.
6. "Poor man," the professor thinks, "I hope my glasses make his life a little easier."

Chapter 14.
A WORK OF ART

Exercise II

1.	b	4.	c
2.	a	5.	b
3.	c	6.	c

Exercise III

1. Sasha's mother buys old furniture and art.
2. Nobody knows where the second one is.
3. He does not want to hurt Sasha and his mother.
4. Igor is not married and lives alone. or/ Dr. Rostov decides that the work of art is a perfect present for an unmarried man.
5. Nikita and his actor friends are always having wild parties and doing wild things.
6. The women holding up the lamp are too fat.

ABOUT THE AUTHOR

For many years, Judith Bailey was a teacher, and most particularly, a reading teacher, in the Los Angeles Unified School District. Under an ESAA grant, she worked with hundreds of newly arrived students who spoke little or no English. Books, reading, the whole spectrum of language arts, have been her life-long preoccupation. Before becoming a teacher, she was a story analyst and associate story editor in several motion picture studios.

She now lives in Forestville, California, where she occupies herself as a free lance writer for major educational publishers.

ABOUT THE ARTIST

Carlos Lacámara was born in Cuba, but has lived in other parts of the world, until settling in Los Angeles in the 1960s. He maintains his art studio there, where he works in all media. His great interest is in California history and the West. His work has appeared in *National Geographic* and in other periodicals, and he has had one-man art shows both in the United States and abroad.